WRITING WOMAN ANTHOLOGY:
Drama and Scholarly Essays

An Anthology of African and Asian Writers and Artists

VOL 3

Curated and edited by **Tendai Rinos Mwanaka**
Sue Zhu
Abigail George
Mona Lisa Jena

Cover art by Tendai Rinos Mwanaka

Mwanaka Media and Publishing Pvt Ltd,
Chitungwiza Zimbabwe
*
Creativity, Wisdom and Beauty

Publisher: *Mmap*
Mwanaka Media and Publishing Pvt Ltd
24 Svosve Road, Zengeza 1
Chitungwiza Zimbabwe
mwanaka@yahoo.com
mwanaka13@gmail.com
https://www.mmapublishing.org
www.africanbookscollective.com/publishers/mwanaka-media-and-publishing
https://facebook.com/MwanakaMediaAndPublishing/

Distributed in and outside N. America by African Books Collective
orders@africanbookscollective.com
www.africanbookscollective.com

ISBN: 978-1-77931-464-2
EAN: 9781779314642

© Tendai Rinos Mwanaka 2023

All rights reserved.
No part of this book may be reproduced or transmitted in any form or by any means, mechanical or electronic, including photocopying and recording, or be stored in any information storage or retrieval system, without written permission from the publisher

DISCLAIMER
All views expressed in this publication are those of the author and do not necessarily reflect the views of *Mmap*.

About Editors

Tendai Rinos Mwanaka is a Zimbabwean publisher; a multidisciplinary artist, editor, mentor and thinker with 26 individual books and at least 27 curated and edited anthologies published in Zimbabwe, Cameroon, Northern Ireland, UK, and USA, 2 music albums, hundreds of paintings, drawings, literary pieces and other artworks curated, exhibited and published in over 400 journals in at least 35 countries.

Abigail George is a blogger, essayist, short story writer, screenwriter, novelist, and poet. She has two film projects in development, is the recipient of two grants from the National Arts Council. Her publishers are Mwanaka Media and Publishing or Mmap, Gazebo Books, and Ovi. She was nominated and longlisted for several prizes. "Young Galaxies" (a poetry book) is forthcoming in 2023 from Mmap.

Mona Lisa Jena is an award-winning author, translator from Odisha, in the Eastern part of India. Her poems and stories have been translated into other languages. She has 22 books to her name. She writes both in her mother tongue Odia and in English. She has read her poems at prestigious literary platforms in India and abroad. A committed poet and a writer.

Sue Zhu, is a New Zealand Chinese poet, artist, Continental coordinator of WPM (world poetry movement), extraordinary ambassador of the Naji Naaman literature prize foundation, vice president of NZ Poetry/Art Association, honorary director of the US-China Culture/Art Centre, published 3 children's education books, 2 poetry collections and 1 translation book. Poems of her are translated into over 20 languages, her paintings can be found on the book cover of prestigious anthologies and are collected by people.

Table of Contents

About Editors..iii
Contributor's Bio Notes..v
Introduction..vii
ALONE: BUNMI ADEDINA (Nigeria)...........................1
APOGEE (A suffragette fiasco): Eziwho Emenike Azunwo (Nigeria)..57
Broken Snail: Chika Onyashiyiwa Ose-Agbo (Nigeria)..........106
The Mirage, or The Vast Misenlightenment of Andy Ntia: Itunuoluwa Williams (Nigeria)....................................135
Domestic Violence in Contemporary Nigerian Drama: A Discourse of Julie Okoh's In Our Own Voices: Eziwho Emenike AZUNWO..183
Cultural Influence on Gender Inequality In Osedebamen Oamen's The Women Of Orena Are Wiser Than The Gods: AMIRIHEOBU Frank Ifeanyichukwu, NWARU Chris and CHIMEZIEM Gloria Ernest-Samuel (Nigeria)...................223
Women and Change Expedition in Julie Okoh's Edewede: Eziwho Emenike AZUNWO (Nigeria)..........................252
Mmap Multidisciplinary Series..................................266

Contributor's Bio Notes

Bunmi Adedina is a Senior Lecturer and drama teacher in the Department of Theatre and Performing Arts, Lagos state University of Education, Oto/Ijanikin, (formerly Adeniran Ogunsanya College of Education, Lagos State). Her teaching experience spans over two decades of promoting drama in Education especially at Primary and Secondary schools for learners. She is a seasoned graduate of Theatre Arts from the prestigious University of Ibadan, Nigeria, where she obtained a Diploma, B.A (Hons), M.A and PhD. She is a versatile actor, stage director, writer, talented artist with many scholarly works to her credit.

Dr Eziwho Emenike Azunwo aka Academic Rabbi is a Senior Lecturer at the Rivers State University, P.M.B. 5080, Port Harcourt, Nigeria. He hails from Rundele in Emohua LGA of Rivers State. He was a lecturer at University of Port Harcourt. He is an emerging voice in contemporary Nigerian playwriting with cogent concepts. He has some published plays and many articles; some of his plays include: *Gbuji, Suffering in Paradise, The Last Resort, etc.* One of his articles was classified as one of the 700 articles of the year 2018 by *https://noussommesfans.com/2019/01/06/articles-memoires-et-theses-de-lannee-2018-la-liste/Fan* studies et culture populaire in Paris, France.

Chika Onyashiyiwa Ose-Agbo, Ph.D, teaches at the Department of English and Literary Studies, Federal University of Lafia, Lafia, Nasarawa State, Nigeria. Her research interests include: African literature, proverb studies, gender studies, popular culture and poetry. Her recent publications include: "Alago Proverbs as Vehicles for Values and Virtues", Ahyu: A Journal of Language and Literature (2022), "Nigerian Proverbs as Signposts of Authourity and Education: A Comparative Analysis of Selected Igbo and Alago Proverbs", Jos Journal of Written and Oral Literature (2021) and "Alago Proverbs as Aesthetics and Tools for Rhetorics", Kalangu: Journal of Language and Literary Studies (2021).

Itunuoluwa Williams is a 1st-year Master's student in History at the University of Mississippi, USA. Born and bred in Lagos, Nigeria, Itunuoluwa relocated for higher education studies and received her bachelor's degree in political science. Her specialization is African history and Gender Studies, and her research interests include pre-colonial African cultural history, Body Theory & Fat Studies, girlhood studies, and women representation and girl development in Nigeria.

Introduction

Could this be the golden age of the African Renaissance?

Again Nigeria, the land of milk and honey when it comes to educationalists, universities, intellectualism and quantitative thinkers takes the lead. The palimpsest and tapestry of dramatists and scholars in this volume is energetic, filled with purity of thought, the vessel of intention and opportune vision. The Nigerians are a powerhouse, pioneers invested in storytelling and research within the symbiosis of a genuine reality. The signs and symbols are there on the page of self-transformational agency, access, interchangeable objectivity that quantifies and solidifies the standing of scribes, seers, prophets, and so we contemplated about this novel generation of seekers coming out of Nigeria, coming from the deepest, darkest continent of Africa in chapters and parts, characters oozing influence and meaning, a metaphysical inquiry into the lasting effects of the vestiges of the "historical landmarks" that has touched the blueprint of social justice and inequality, enlightenment and consciousness of dramatists and scholars appearing in the no holds barred landscape of Nigeria. This body of work, this creation boldly searches for the intersection between political scenario and bureaucracy, familial bonds, structures and hierarchies. Each of these cultural practitioners and social anthropologists dive deep into the recesses of the mind.

Over the years, since ancient times there has been ancestral knowledge systems that have defined who we are as scholars and dramatists at the heart of who we are. We were defined by the courage of our warriors on the battlefield, the peaks and troughs in the energetic field. These knowledge systems have helped us transition from an Occidental mode of thinking, to maintain our ministerial norms, values and principles as seekers, scribes, and age old prophets in this novel era. This mindset alongside the African methodology, existentialism and phenomenology has stood the test of time. As far as we are concerned our belief systems and psychological framework has not changed on the African continent when it comes to fable and folklore steeped in history, the tradition and heritage of oral storytelling and mythology. Both dramatist and scholar take sands of time, the mysterious hands of the clock, illustrious knowledge, and the nuclear family into their stride. With each thread complementing memory and gut symmetry, the phantasmagorical forecast of primordial soup in melting pot, the juxtapositioning of ideologies following the natural efficiency and exponential consistency of what is trending, the hallucinogenic and psychedelic symbolism, signs and symbolism this continent has to offer. Personal ethics, infinite intelligence and self-improvement also have a hand in turning these texts and flow of ideas from African soil into a narrative on the Promised Land.

Discontent, "kingdom", the science of the family in Africa, there is the interplay of social issues, principled justice, societal norms, what we consider commodity and atomic value since ancient times, the search for meaning, spirit in these pages.

We grasp Bunmi Adedina's play "Alone" through fables, folklore and parables. It is a representation as are the other works of Nigeria "in continual flux". The writing is fluid and complex, the scale is visionary and dense, sparse morsel and yet food for thought that nurtures and provides sustenance, attention is paid in microscopic detail to place, location, location, location, space whether it is creative or justified. The spotlight falls on the question of gender based violence, gender inequality, cultural favour and influence. You strike a woman, you strike a rock. Eziwho Emenike Azunwo, the curiously inventive title "Broken Snail" by Chika Onyashiyiwa Ose-Agbo, "The Mirage, or The Vast Misenlightenment of Andy Ntia" by Itunuoluwa Williams, "Domestic Violence in Contemporary Nigerian Drama: A Discourse of Julie Okoh's In Our Own Voices" by Eziwho Emenike Azunwo starts us off in this volume. Writing for writers. The writers in this volume are trailblazers, setting an impactful and sequential course in action and with their expertise they are not only advocates or rather setting up literal "force-shields" and predetermined advocacy bodies, they are history in the making on the face of this continent marking time in the global arena. This is the golden age for dramatists coming out of Africa. Essayists, researchers and scholars have been establishing their opinions since ancient times, interpreting contemporary society.

We adapt. Africa has always adapted. Europe is the museum of the world filled with empty palaces, and if America is the Prozac Nation of the world, filled with poverty, scarcity, self-help and personal development gurus, despair, discontent at all levels in society, dis-ease, economic recession, the powerful celebrity of Trump and the spotlight firmly centered on a reality television driven era, a population that finds life meaningless and without purpose if they are not driven by materialism, material worth, then they are driven by a poor mindset and a non-substantive paradigm of their psychic and intuitive beliefs and systems. Whereas Africa has the upper hand when it comes to the modus operandi of the signs and symbolism of spirit and spirituality and ancestral knowledge and worship. There is a ministry and anointing on these pages, the understanding of the reality within, intense quantum states of thinking that is fundamental to our conscious mode of thinking, our progress, our forward-moving processes. We speak our truth into existence, we write our truth into history and we are the self-transformative change that we want to see in the world. We are atoms conceived, formed, shaped by a psychic, intuitive frequency and vibration in our bloodline and informed by molecular structure. The scholars and dramatists herein are made of physics. There is something alchemical, physical, radioactive as the reader's intellect meets the intellect on the page. We have the interwoven fabric of stars here, coming into alignment at certainly the beginning of their careers. Watch out for these voices, the vibrations that they complement and the frequencies in which they operate. They will stand the test of the "narrow passage" of time. We salute all of you.

ALONE
BUNMI ADEDINA

DRAMATIS PERSONAE

Papa	- Storyteller
Edu	- Odum's Husband
Odum	- Edu's Wife
Obi	- Village Head of Umugwu
Obidia	- Obi's wife
Adaobi	- Obi's Daughter
Akunma	- Adaobi's friend
Igwe Akachi	- King of Akagaa
Emeka	- Igwe's son
Old man	- Edozie's foster father
Edozie	- Odum's Son
Owan	- Priest
Chiefs	- Okonkwo, Orji, Uche, Udo,
Umu Ada	- Oyinsi (Leader), Ijeoma, Urechi, Ugo, Eririnma, Ogenma, Ngozi Ekenma, Nonso, Adaugo
Ogwo's family	- Dede, Umunna, Ifeanyi. Keke
Nwankwo's family	- Adindu, Eyinna

Nkume — *Obi's Guard*

Village Children — *Dike, Obinna, Amaka, Adaugo, Oluchi, Emeka, Ebere, Nnamdi*

Villagers — *1ˢᵗ Woman, 2ⁿᵈ Woman, Man, Orienma, Afonma*

Youths, Crowd, Dancers

OPENING

It is evening. Lights come up on a village square. Children are involved in diverse activities, singing, wrestling, dancing and so on, almost concurrently. Later, an elderly man comes in without being noticed by the children. He observes them for a while then calls.

Papa:
Akuko
Children:
(They all respond) Uto uwa.
Papa:
(Calls again) Akuko
Children:
(They all respond) Uto uwa.
Papa:
My dear children
Children:
Good evening Papa

Nnamdi:
(Quickly brings in a stool) Papa sit down
Papa:
Thank you. Nnamdi, my, son. How are you? How is your father?
Nnamdi:
He is feeling better now, Papa
Papa:
Obinna, I hope you helped your mother at home today
Obinna:
Yes papa, I gathered sticks for her from the farm
Ebere:
Papa I'm here too
Children:
Papa I'm here too
Papa:
Okay. Okay, all of you, how are you my children?
Children:
Fine papa
Papa:
Let us sing our song (He starts a song and the children join. There's much noise and excitement)
Papa:
It's okay, settle down
Obinna:
Papa tell us a story
Children:
Yes, yes, yes
Emeka:
Yes tell us about the elephant

Amaka:
No, tell us about the dog
Chikodi:
Tell us about the cat
Papa:
I know the story to tell you tonight. In three days' time we will be celebrating Odum festival. Children do you know why we celebrate Odum festival every year?
Children:
No, papa
Dike:
Why is Odum festival so special?
Papa:
Ok, I will tell you today. Odum festival in preparation and anticipation of harvest season. Many people seize the opportunity to resolve conflicts and settle quarrels for peaceful co-existence before harvest. It is held in remembrance of the great deeds of a woman who saved Umugwu and brought peace to our land.
Children:
From what Papa?
Papa:
Don't be in a haste. Today's story will be told in a special way. I would like, every one of you to participate. So, you will be taking up roles as the story unfolds.
Children:
Yeeeees
Adaugo:
I will play the beautiful girl
Children:

No, no
Emeka:
I am handsome so I will marry the beautiful girl
Amaka:
Who told you the story is about a beautiful girl and her husband? Papa says the story is about Odum festival
Papa:
Yes, children, today's story is about a great woman of this very village. Her name is Odumnaka. Oluchi I hope the costumes are washed
Oluchi:
Yes Papa, but we are yet to bring in new costumes on Afo market day as earlier agreed (*there is general consent*)
Papa:
Don't worry, our audience will understand. They know you (*to the audience*) or don't you? (*audience are to respond*). You see, so, go ahead. Now Oluchi, go and bring our bag. We will use available costume and props. The most important thing in this story is the message (*children are happy and start going about their business. Oluchi distributes costumes to some of the children*). (*To the audience*) Please sit back and watch our performance. These children you see are not professionals. They're only villagers taking up roles as actors. But I assure you they will give you their very best (*back to children*). My children I can see that you're all ready. Settle down and let the story unfold. Once upon a time, in a faraway land... (*Screams and shouts are heard off stage. A loud fearful sound is heard. Children on stage immediately disperse joining the pandemonium of people running helter scatter*).

DISPUTE

Scene takes place in front of Edu's house. Lights come up on a couple

Odum:
(*Trying to block his way*). Edum you are not going anywhere

Edu:
Woman, what is the problem with you?

Odum:
I say no. You cannot give them the only inheritance of your father

Edu:
They promised to give us another land in a better location

Odum:
No, you are not giving that land out

Edu:
Odum, the village has more need of the land and they promise to give us another land near Orji river. I think that will be better for us my dear wife

Odum:
That is what they told you? That is what you think? This same people will use it against you later on. It will become a parable that you relinquished the only inheritance your father left for you.

Edu:
Woman, watch it! Who is the man of the house? Who is the husband here?

Odum:
I am sorry Chinedu my husband. What I am saying is for our own good, our future

Edu:

I thought you always advocated collective good for all

Odum:

Yes, and I still do. Sometimes you need to detach from the crowd and be alone so you can see clearly. This land is our only hope. Our opening into the future. My husband, please don't jeopardise our chance for future happiness.

Edu:

Okay, come, sit down. In clear terms, give me one genuine reason why I shouldn't exchange the land

Odum:

Edu I can't tell you now, but please try and listen to me. My reasons are best known to me.

Edu:

You see. The same old response. My wife, I love you and you know I truly do but I refuse to be a weakling just because of some unknown fear for the future. I am ready for whatever comes my way.

Odum:

Please Dimu oma, let the village look for another land.

Edu:

Woman, if truly I am your husband in this house, then my word is final. That land I inherited from my father now belongs to the village. (Exits)

Odum:

Edum Please. Chimoooooo (She keeps crying and wailing)

SISTERHOOD

A gathering of women known as Umu Ada, at the village square. Lights come up as women come in and take their seats.

Oyinsi:
Ndewo nu. Greetings dear sisters. Odum we got your message, it was rather too urgent

Odum:
I am so sorry for bothering you. I know it is not time for our monthly meeting. I can also see that not all umu Ada are present. This is a matter that cannot wait. Please pardon me. This is my fine for calling this emergency meeting (*hands over an amount of money to Oyinsi*)

Oyinsi:
Umu Ada, this is your kola

Women:
We are grateful

Oyinsi:
Odum talk, we are all one and we are here already

Odum:
Nde Ada, has there been any time I've neglected my obligations to the women

Women:
No

Odum:
My friends, is there a time I've never stepped in to solve other people's problems?

Eririnma:

You are the one that saved me from my husband's constant beating, if not he will still be pounding me like fufu.

Ugo:
It was your timely intervention that saved me, if not my husband would have sent me away and married that girl with a flat nose

Urechi:
Odumnaka, it was your advice that helped me, if not my husband's people would have sent me and my children away, so that they can take over his property after his death.

Ijeoma:
What is it you want to say? Say it Odum, we are here for you

Odum:
Thank you very much my sisters, 1 like this show of love and genuine concern. May God continue to bless you all.

All:
I see

Odum:
Now I know that we are truly sisters. Do you remember that my husband's only land I told you about?

All:
Yes, we do

Odum:
Thank you. My husband is still insisting on giving that, our only land, to the village

Ogenma:
Why, why?

Odum:

He doesn't seem to see reason with me at all. He has now given his consent and the youths of this town will be there to clear it next Eke

All:
Mba nu! Impossible

Odum:
That is why I've called you. Help me. Save me my sisters

Oyinsi:
These men are all the same. Why are they always so stubborn?

Ngozi:
I'd rather say unreasonable. They will stop at nothing to suppress us

Ekenma:
They also complain that we women are difficult to understand.

Ugo:
It is only because they are not patient with us

Ijeoma:
Women are the easiest going creatures on earth. We only become difficult when men remold us into what we are not.

Ogenma:
Show a woman love, you get love. Show a woman hate, you get hell in return.

All:
Exactly

Oyinsi:
That is why we must be strong. That is the only time we can support one another. We must not allow bickering and backbiting to divide us. Back to the issue on ground. How do we help our friend and sister Odum?

Ngozi:
I have an idea, let's get some boys from nearby village to lay ambush and to beat the youths up

Urechi:
No, we have agreed in our meetings that we will not use violence to resolve issues. We rely more on brains than brawn.

Odum:
So what do we do?

Ekenma:
Let us use mask to scare them away.

Odum:
Mask will never work in this case. Remember the case of Akachi. (*Ijeoma whispers in Oyinsi's ear*). Ijeoma, thank you. Sisters, come closer, the wall has ears.

Lights out

SOLIDARITY

Scene takes place on a portion of land somewhere in the village. Some young men arrive with cutlasses, hoes, spades etc to clear the land. There is general talk and singing. Two women enter from same direction. The youths stop to greet them.

Ijeoma:
Well done my sons. What are you all doing here so early?

Nonso:
We're running an errand for the village. We're to clear this land as our new market (*three other women enter from other directions*)

Adaugo:
Did I just hear you say this is our new market site??

Chike:
Yes Nne. In fact we are determined to finish clearing it before sunset today

Ugonna:
Oh that is very good, well done my children (*Odum and another woman enter from another direction. Youths greet them too*)

Odum:
Well done, my sons

Ijeoma:
They are here to clear this land as our new market site.

Odum:
Oh I see, this is indeed good news. May you also be rewarded for this act of obedience

Youths:
Thank you our mothers

Ndube:

Let's get to work

Odum:
Women. Let's go too, if not the market will be empty before we get there. Goodbye my children. (*Women greet youths but secretly pour the contents of their hidden containers in the air where the youths are. They take their leave thereafter*).

Chike:
There's too much sun fly in this place (*scratching his body*)

Ndube:
That's good observation I didn't want to be the first to speak

Nonso:
Help, my back. Please scratch this side for me

Chike:
No, noo... this is... I'm going to die (*there is sudden commotion as youths scream, scratch and roll on the floor crying for help. They finally disperse in diverse directions*).

Lights out.

LOVERS

An isolated spot hidden from public view. Adaobi and her friend Akunna are chatting

Adaobi:

I'm getting tired of this long wait

Akunma:

Me too. (*Listening*) I think I hear footsteps. (*Goes to check but comes back disappointed*). Oh no, I was wrong.

Adaobi:

Let's go home

Akunma;

I think so too. (*A handsome young man sneaks in and tiptoes to Adaobi covering her Eyes from behind*)

Adaobi:

(*Happy to see him but feigns annoyance*). I am going home

Edozie:

My love, I am truly sorry. Please forgive me. I missed the first trip. Had to join the second canoe

Adaobi:

But you have always made it early before

Edozie:

I know. My father is old and I had to run some errands for him before coming. Adaobi my love, please forgive me. (*They both embrace*)

Akunma:

(*Coughs*) I shall go and keep watch but please don't keep long.

Adaobi:

We won't

Akunma:

(Reluctant to leave) Adaobi, I think you need to...

Adaobi:
Don't worry, I'm okay

Akunma:
Let me sit here then.

Edozie:
Akunna, thank you very much. I appreciate your support. *(pushing her to leave)*

Akunma:
Thank you, but I want to...

Adaobi:
Enough of this, Akun. Now, go *(Pushes her out gently)*

Edozie;
My love, I have missed you so much

Adaobi:
But we just saw last Eke market day

Edozie;
A day without seeing you is more than a season put together

Adaobi:
Don't tease me

Edozie:
My love, my beauty, my queen

Adaobi:
Don't flatter me

Edozie:
It is true. And that is why I can't wait to have you as my wife.
(Adaobi is silent).
Edozie:
What is it my love?
Adaobi:
That talk... It's...
Edozie:
But you yourself told me that your father is planning to marry you off before the end of the harvest. Or are you only deceiving me? You have given your consent then?
Adaobi:
Dozie, that's not it. I am not interested in Emeka one bit. I know he's from a royal home and wealthy. Exactly my father's spec of a husband for me. But I don't love him. Unfortunately.my father insists I must marry him to foster his relationship with
Igwe.
Edozie:
Have you talked to mother about it?
Adaobi:
I have severally but her words are not comforting at all. She says I must obey Papa just like she obeyed hers by marrying my father. She says young girls have no say in matters like this. She says …
Edozie:
And what do you say?
Adaobi:
I say… It's too difficult for me, Dozie. I don't know what to do anymore.
Edozie:

Then you have agreed to marry Emeka?
Adaobi:
Tufia kwa!
Edozie:
You still want to marry me, don't you?
Adaobi:
Yes, of course
Edozie:
Elope with me, my love. Let's go to a faraway land where no one can find us. Where we'll forever be happy.
Adaobi:
That doesn't sound nice. It's not as easy as that. Moreover, there's more I can't tell you now.
Edozie:
So, we now have secrets? (*Feigns anger*)
Akunma:
(*Rushes in*) Hide, hide, someone's coming (*Edozie hides somewhere then Akunnma suddenly burst into laughter*)
Adaboi:
What is it?
Akunma:
I'm lonely
Adaobi:
Please Akunma, do this for me, we're almost through
Akunma:
Promise?
Adaobi:
Yes promise (calls) Dozie come out, there's no one in view. Akunma only played a fast one on us

Edozie:
Oh! I understand, Akunma take this I shall bring more for you next Eke (*gives her some Udala fruits from his bag*).

Akunma:
Are these all for me?

Edozie:
Yes

Akunma:
Oh thank you very much, can I come and...

Adaobi:
Now you can go (*pushes her out*) time is running out. (*Akunma leaves reluctantly*). Dozie, I will have to leave soon.

Edozie:
Alright, no more talk of marriage and eloping today. Okay? I composed a song for you

Adaobi:
Another one?

Edozie:
And many yet to come. Listen to it (*Edozie sings and other players join. Edozie and Adaobi dance for a while. Suddenly, Adaobi gives a piercing scream and falls down. Amidst confusion, Akunma rushes in*)

Akunma:
What is it? (sees *Adaobi lying still*)

Edozie:
(*Calling*) Adaobi, my love, my queen, my.....

Akunma:
Adaobi, Ada... Quick let's take her home.

Edozie:
Have you forgotten? I must not be sighted in this land.

Akunma:
Don't worry. Just help me get her to the village square. Leave the rest to me. This way. (*Edozie carries her out*)
Lights out.

KINDRED

The scene takes place in Dede's compound. A family meeting of Ogwo and Nwankwo

Dede:
Cha, cha,cha, kwenu
All:
Heee
Dede:
Kwezuenu
All:
Heee
Dede:
Ndewo nu. Greetings to you all my people, especially our in-laws from Umugwu. This is kola. He that brings kola brings life
All:
Yes Nnayin
Dede:
To say that we are surprised at your call for this sitting, is a lie. Notwithstanding, we will allow you to state your case before we know what to do. My people, have I spoken well?
All:
Very well indeed, Dede
Adindu:
Thank you De anyi. You all know me. I am Adindu, head of Nwakwo's family. Our elders say, if you see an elderly man running in broad daylight, if he's not chasing something, then, something must be chasing him.
Eyinna:

That is true, Nnayin
Adindu:
Also, when a child cuts trees in the forest, it's only an elder that knows the direction it will fall
Dede:
It is true. We thank you once more but you have only been speaking in parables so far. Tell us exactly where all these is leading to
Ifeanyi:
Yes, please go straight to the point and stop beating about the bush
Keke:
Or are you not man enough to say what is on your mind?
Eyinna:
I demand an apology for this insult from Ifeanyi to the head of our family
Keke:
I was actually expecting you to talk. Remember, we still have unfinished business. You, traitor
Eyinna:
And I am ready for you today. You that your father never had a roof over his head till he died
Keke:
(*Rising up in anger*) Elders, did you hear that?
Adindu:
Taa, keep quiet Eyinna. Such words are too heavy for your mouth.
Eyinna:
But you heard him. He started it and you didn't stop him
Keke:

I will say whatever I want to say and there is nothing you can do about it

(*The confrontation increases as family members take sides*)

Dede:
Quiet. Quiet all of you. What has the world turned to? Little children that cannot clean the mucus on their nose standing up to elders.

Umunna:
Forgive them, Dede

Adindu:
The world is upside down

Dede:
Anyone that distrupts this meeting will pay a fine of a he goat.

Eyinna:
Forgive me, Nnayin

Keke:
I am sorry my elders.

Dede:
In addition, I will arrange a wrestling bout for Keke and Eyinna since they're both bent on flexing their muscles. That way, you will have to settle your differences permanently.

Keke:
Dede, it has not gotten to that. Ifeanyi and I are friends. It's just a little disagreement.

Eyinna:
Yes, Nnayin, We're very good friends. (*Goes to embrace Keke*) see?

Dede:

You better be because any other unsolicited word from either of you will keep you away from this discussion. Please continue our in-law, Adindu

Adindu:
Thank you Nnayin. We are here because of the lingering issue between our son, Chinedu and your daughter Odumnaka. If you permit me, I will like Edu to shed light on the matter.

Dede:
Chinedu, go ahead

Edu:
Thank you Nnayin. I greet all family members of Ogwo, both old and young, Nnayin Adindu and all members of Nwankwo family where I hail from. My wife, Odum, now insists on being the husband while I remain the wife.

All:
Tufia kwa! Abomination!

Edu:
I seceded my portion of land inherited from my father to my village to build a new market because it is central. This was not an easy decision for me too but after so many pleas from Obi and Ndichie, I had no choice. Particularly as it will be in the interest of majority. A new market will bring about development, economic boom to our village and grant access to other neighbouring towns and villages for further interactions and exchange of goods and services. All these I calmly explained to Odum but my wife says no. And she has gone ahead to take actions to truncate this arrangement with Umu Ada. This is why I am here with my kindred as a sign of respect, to appeal that you call her to order before the matter gets out of hand. I have arrived. Thank you all.

Umunna:
Hmmmm. Dede, this is indeed a huge matter. But I believe a rat does not run out of its hole in broad daylight unless there is fire

Dede:
That is true. Odum is our good daughter though we all know she can be stubborn for a just cause. Her late father, my uncle called me on several occasions to speak to her. So, this is not a surprise to us. Chinedu, we have heard all you said and will send for her to find out the rationale for her actions. I promise you that this issue would be resolved amicably. Does anybody have anything to add?

Adindu:
You have spoken well Nnayin.

Ifeanyi:
My elders, I was just thinking

Dede:
What?

Ifeanyi:
Why would a man readily give up his only inheritance from his father to build a village market? I think it is rather…

Dede:
You're not thinking anything here, Ifeanyi. It is not your land neither is it your father's land. The land in question belongs to Edu and he has the right to do as he chooses with it. Final.

Keke:
But, Nnanyi, what of his lineage, generations after him

Eyinna:
Exactly. There is no generation after him. (*Cynically*) And we all know the reason for that. The truth is bitter but must be told.

Keke:

Watch your mouth. *(There is dead silence)*.

Adindu:
I will not sit and watch a child poke fingers in my eyes. Dede, we have spoken our mind and we have heard your response. We await further actions from you.

Edu:
I thank you all and apologise for inconveniences. I am the yam that soiled your hands with oil.

Dede:
(Calling) Isioma, Isioma, bring the food. We are done with discussions.

Eyinna:
That will not be necessary. We already ate to our fill before we left home Nnayin. Thank you for your hospitality.

Adindu:
My in-laws, we take our leave now. *(He exits with Edu and Eyinna)*

Dede:
Go well our in-laws. *(Pause to look at Ifeanyi and Keke then enters his inner room)*

(Umunna rises, looks at Ifeanyi and Keke shaking his head. He leaves without saying a word. Ifeanyi and Keke remain seated looking at each other).

Ifeanyi:
What? Somebody cannot talk again?

Keke:
Your mouth stinks.

Lights Out.

VERDICT

The village square. A gong is heard in the distance. The town crier's voice announces his entrance on stage. By now a crowd has gathered.

Nkwo:
Ge nu nti. Listen very well. I am only a messenger I have no word of my own. All I am going to say is exactly the way I was, told. Ge nu nti…

1st woman:
Nkwo, what exactly is the message?

Nkwo:
Sshh… woman don't shout at me. I am not your husband

2nd woman:
All she is saying is, give us the message from Obi

Nkwo:
I can see that all of you women have now grown mustache and you want to be equal to men. No wonder your husbands can no longer control you at home.

3rd woman:
Look, Nkwo, watch your tongue. Have you come here to abuse us? That is why no woman ever agreed to marry you.

Nkwo:
He he he (*Laughing*). Yes, because I am too good for them and I will not take any rubbish from any woman

1st Woman:
Please let's allow him deliver the message. He has taken more than his fill at the palm wine stand (*general laughter*)

Nkwo:
Okay, if that is the way you want it. Obi and the elders of Ediaba warn everybody in the land and advise you in your own interest

not to have anything to do with Odumnaka wife of Chinedu. Do not greet her. Do not answer her greeting. Do not sell to her and do not buy from her. Do not take from her and do not give to her. Anyone, especially you women that disobeys this instruction will face the music. And I hope that this will teach all of you women to respect me. Ge nu ntiiiii… (*Nkwo goes out. There is general consternation and various reactions to the news. As villagers disperse Orienma and Afonma discuss*)

Orienma:
Chai, poor woman! What did she do to deserve this type of punishment?

Afonma:
Arrogance. Pride. Stubbornness. No wonder God blocked her womb from…

Orienma:
(*Covers her mouth*). Ssshh, that's a bad thing to say about your fellow woman.

Afonma:
I don't care. If you like associate with her. You know what awaits you (*Leaves*)

Orienma:
Odum, may your Chi vindicate you. Afo, wait for me.

Lights Out.

THE DREAM

Odumnaka is seen lying on a mat in her house. A woman appears to her in a dream. All actions here appear like a trance

Mama:

Odumnaka, rise and listen to me my daughter

Odum:

Mama, it's you again

Mama:

Yes my child. This is the time to act. Adaobi is in her inactive stage again. Go now and get Osan leaves from your husband's land. Do with it as you have been instructed earlier on and the menace, of the beast will stop. Remember this is the only key to your future happiness. You will no longer be barren and you also shall be addressed as a mother. But remember no single soul must hear of this until you have accomplished this task.

Odum:

But mama....

Mama:

I take my leave. You shall no longer see me in this form. Do as you as you're told and you will be happy. Go now. (*Odumnaka wakes up to find out that it is a dream*).

Odum:

Mama, mama… Osan leaves…A dream….

Lights Out

SOLITUDE

Women of the land assemble to discuss issues relating to them at the village square

Oyinsi:
So, it is a general consensus that the sweeping of the village square be left to Ure's age group. While the clearing of the stream and environs be the duty of all the women.

Women:
Yes

Ekenma:
Do not forget the clearing of the new market site in a fortnight from new. That is the only way the entire village will know that we are in full support.

Ogenma:
Also, remember that we are all expected to come along with some refreshment for the men. *(Odum enters. The women are quiet)*

Odum:
Women of Ediaba. Greeting to you all. *(No response)*. Has my greeting become a taboo to you too Umu Ada? You promised to stay by me through thick and thin as I have done for many of you. Remember, the rain falls on all, both the good and the bad. I am the one affected today. Who knows? It might be you tomorrow.

When danger is at your heels it is to the house you run to for shelter. So I have come to you, my sisters and my friends. You said we should always be strong together. Umuada, I need your support. I am doing this for all of us. Please, don't disown me too. Don't turn your backs on me. *(There's total silence as women move and maintain a distance from Odum holding their lips tight. Finally, Odum leaves).*

Ijeoma:
Fellow women, let us reconsider our stand in Odum's case. After all she is one of us.

Oyinsi:
Are you out of your mind?

Eririnma:
Do you realize the implication of what you're asking us to do?

Ngozi:
Please I am not ready to be sent packing to my parents' house. Each and every one of us know the extent our husbands will go if we disobey.

Ijeoma:
Husbands. Always our husbands. Our lives does not depend on them.

Eririnma:
Yes, we know. We must have a voice but there are restrictions

Ijeoma:
We can break free from these restrictions and still be a good wife and mother

Oyinsi:
It's easier said than done, Ijeoma. You can only win a battle well prepared for. And even at that there will be causalities. It will take a while so we must tread softly.

Urechi:
There is no going back. Let Odum respect her husband and the entire village. Anyway, whether she likes it or not the new market will still be on her husband's land.

Ugo:
Yes, we cannot all stop existing because of one single individual. Our market is a major source of income to us. It is what we are well known for in this neighbourhood.
Eririnma:
Even our children's children will not forgive us if we allow her to be a stumbling block.
Ugo:
Talking about children, we all know she doesn't have a child of her own. So, how will she consider other people's children?
Oyinsi:
Stop. I say stop. Ugonna, That is not a good thing to say about a sister. If we cannot help her in her time of need, then we must not compound her problems.
Ijeoma:
Friends, I agree with all you've said, Odumnaka has never let any of us down in our time of need. All I am saying is...
Ugo:
Oyinsi has spoken well. We may not be able to help Odum in this instance.
Oyinsi:
We shall not speak on this matter again. We will meet again on Orie market day. Remember the assigned tasks. (*there's an awkward silence as Oyinsi leaves. Other women leave one after the other too. Ijeoma stays back*)
Odum:
(*Odum sneaks in*) Ijeoma, your friends have all left. Won't you join them?
Ijeoma:

(*Looking round cautiously*) Odum, I don't want to talk to you. It is a sacrifice too great for anyone to make. Look go and apologize to the whole village and ask for forgiveness so that the gods will smile on you.

Odum:
Thank you my friend. I can now see that true friendship knows no bounds. On the issue of the land, I will not relent. I shall do all within my power to stop this project. As for the gods, they stopped smiling on me a long time ago

Ijeoma:
Why? Why are you doing this to yourself? Just apologise and…

Odum:
Apologise? For what offence? I would rather die than apologize. After all, I am doing all these for the village. If this is how they will pay me back, then I leave the gods to judge. I will stand up to the whole village alone and I shall prevail. You will see.

Ijeoma:
Odum you sound strange and foreign to me

Odum:
So did great women of old sound. They fought lone battles. But they conquered.

Ijeoma:
They fought for just causes.

Odum:
So, you also believe I am fighting an unjust cause. You? My best friend?

Ijeoma:
I am sorry Odum. I've always known you to be resolute. I know you're right in your own way. I wish I can join in fighting this

battle with you but, I don't understand. Please my friend, be reasonable.

'Odum:
Good. Now that you have said that, please, Ijeoma, take this leaf burn it in a pot and leave it outside your house, in the compound and even your farm lands

Ijeoma;
Odum, go home and take care of yourself. You need rest. I will see you some other time. (*goes out hurriedly*)

Odum:
Ijeoma, believe me I know what I'm doing. I can't explain now. Take it please.

(*Two young boys walk in*)

Odum:
Welcome my, children

1ˢᵗ Boy:
Don't talk to her, she is the one.

2ⁿᵈ Boy:
You mean the cursed woman

1ˢᵗ Boy:
Yes. What do we do now?

Odum:
Even if you will not talk to me please take this leaves, burn it in a pot and leave it outside in front of your house. Help me, I want to be a mother too.

Boys:
(*Screaming*) Help, help, help, (*they run away, other villagers come along and behave in like manner. Finally, Odum is frustrated and starts crying*).

Suddenly there are shouts and screams as people run helter skelter on stage. Commotion persists)
1ˢᵗ man:
Run, run, it's coming this way (*two men rush in*)
2ⁿᵈ man:
I heard the sound, it was like thunder
1ˢᵗ man:
There is no time to talk. Death is right behind you
Odumnaka:
(She approaches them). Here, take. Burn it and place in front of your houses
1ˢᵗ man:
She's mad. Run for your dear lives.
Odumnaka:
(*Sits on the floor, crying*) Please, take it. I' not mad. Please…
(*Loud fearful sounds come up again as more come on stage. There is noise and disarray as people run in different directions. The fearful sound continues as light fades)*
Lights Out.

REVELATION

Obi and elders of the land are in a meeting. There is side talk and some other stage activities

Okonkwo:

Thank you Obi. May your days be long. As we all know, the matter before us is one that has defied remedy. The constant attack of the invisible beast in our land is creating untold hardship in the land.

Udo:

That is not all. Apart from destroying our farm produce and barns. The beast has also been taking a virgin during each attack since the past three years.

Uche:

We can no longer sit and fold our arms. A chronic illness demands a hard cure.

Obi:

My people, you are all aware of the steps we have taken in the past three years since this evil-occurrence started. Which god have we not appeased? What ritual have we not performed? Yet to no avail. The presence of Owaneti in our midst is not by chance. I have invited him here again today to tell us the cause and remedy of this evil wind. Over to you Owan, the all seeing

Owan:

I am a man of few words. The cause is with you, it is in your midst. There is no sacrifice or remedy needed.

Edu:

Are we then to live in constant fear and uncertainty? This year alone, the beast has attacked thrice and we're just in the sixth month. Very soon the harvest season will begin. We will hardly have enough to eat not to talk of selling to neighboring villages.

Okonkwo:

Even our market that used to be our major source which brought us fame in years past is now a shadow of itself. The new market too is now abandoned.

Uche:

Don't talk of the market at all. What do you expect when a mere woman now has the balls of her husband in her hands…

Orji:

He will certainly do his bidding

Edu:

I thogh twe are here to find a lasting solution to the problem of the beast and not to point accusing fingers.

Orji:

Let us call a spade a spade. Edu you are part of our problems in this village

(*there is disagreement among the elders*)

Edu:

What else do you want me to do? I gave my land and now I've sacrificed my wife. Are you never tired of taking?

Udo:

Edu, don't take it that way. Let us...

Edu:

Yes, go on, go ahead and find solutions to your problems but leave my land out of this. From now on, I renounce my membership as council elders Obi, I take my leave (He makes to leave)

Obi:
Stop. Chinedu... Please sit down. Edu is a true son of the soil. He has proven this through his actions. Let us not digress from our main concern of the day. Let us listen to what Owan has to say.

Owan:
Caution, Obioha, caution is the word no one puts hot yam in the mouth and talks with ease. The issue of the land must be approached with caution.

Uche:
What is he saying?

Orji:
Caution. (*Spitefully*)

Owan:
The solution to the attacks is in your midst. But my children caution

Okonkwo:
Told us just a few minutes ago that the cause is with us now you say again that the cure is with us. Old one, you are confusing us.

Owan:
Obi, I will send the herbs for Adaobi, and remember, caution is the word. Goodbye elders of Ediaba *(leaves)*

Orji:
Caution indeed

Obi:
Well, we have all heard with our ears. Let each and every one of us search ourselves. I pray that the gods will guide us.

All:

I see

Obi:
My daughter Adaobi will be getting married to Emeka, son of Igwe Akachi in three weeks from now. You are all invited.

Orji:
Obi, I thought it was scheduled for next harvest season.

Obi:
Yes, but Owan says marrying her off will bring a permanent cure to her constant illness.

Uche:
This is good news. There is something to celebrate after all

Udo:
We better start our own arrangements since we have little time. Fellow elders I beg to take my leave. I am going to see my in-laws in Ndobi (Chiefs *leaves*)

Obi:
(Calls) Obidia (no response) Obidia

Obidia:
Answer from within) Nna anyi *(comes out from the inner room)* I'm here

Obi:
Take your seat. How is she now?

Obidia:
She's okay as usual. She is now fully awake. I gave her water and she has requested for her normal fufu and utazi soup.

Obi:
Yet this ailment has defiles all cure

Obidia:
(Weeping) Nnanyi! Please do something, she is our only hope. She must not die.

Obi:
Don't cry again. We have already taken a step in the right direction. Once she is married this strange illness will stop.

Obidia:
I pray so. This past three years of Adaobi's illness have been full of torture for me

Obi:
That is why we have to make haste. The wedding is in three markets. Owan advised that there should be no further delay. Akachi has already been intimated of the new arrangement.

Obidia:
I heard that he has sent for his son Emeka from the city.

Obi:
If I had not delayed this long, Adaobi would probably be nursing a child by now.

Obidia:
It is not too late, let me go and inform her. I also need to start the wedding arrangements. We have little time.

Obi:
Tell Nkume to bring that stupid boy

Obidia:
Yes, Nna anyi (*a few seconds later, a stern looking young man comes in with Edozie*)

Obi:
Young man, What did you say your mission was?

Dozie:
I came to see Adaobi. I heard she was ill.

Obi:

Where are you from? Who are your parents? I don't ever want to set my eyes on you again. Keep away from Adaobi. You are not fit for her. She's bethroted to the son of Igwe Akachi and arrangements are already in full gear for the wedding.

Dozie:
But I love her. I love Adaobi

Nkume:
Keep quiet

Obi:
Heed my advice for you and your parents' sake. Don't ever set your feet in this land again. Take him away from here.

Dozie:
Let me see her, please. Adaobi my love, my queen (*keeps shouting as Nkume carries him out*).

Obi:
Stupid boy.
Lights Out.

WEDDING

Setting is Obi's courtyard. There is festivity in the air, dance, music and entertainment is going on. Adaobi is led out of the inner chambers by her friends amidst singing).

Orji:

Thank you my people. You are all welcome to this great occasion. It is great because it is a day that every father and mother prays to witness. May you all witness such occasions too.

Villagers:

I seeeee

Orji:

We all know our reason for gathering. Without further delay I will now hand over to the Obi for the final phase of the ceremony.

Obi:

I greet you all my people. Today is a great day for me. I thank you for your support since we started this occasion today. For your information, all that custom law and tradition demand have been duly fulfilled by my in laws. Igwe Akachi has been my bosom friend since our childhood days. And 1 am happy that the union of our children will further strengthen not only our friendship but also the ties between his town and our village in times to come. Please lead my daughter forward. (Adaobi is led forward by her friends)

Obi:

Adaobi my daughter, today is a day of joy for you, wipe your tears. You know that your mother and I love you so much and want the best for you. As you move into your new home may God be with you. You will have children in dozens and you will bring good luck to your husband. And may we your parents never regret this day. (*Handing Adaobi over to Emeka*).

Obi:
Emeka my son, take my daughter Adaobi as your wife. I have no doubt in my mind that you will take good care of her.

Igwe:
Greetings to you my people. Thank you for honouring me on this great occasion of my son's wedding to Adaobi, my friend's daughter. Some friends are more than blood brothers. This is how I rate my friendship with Obioha. I am convinced that we shall still share a lot in common. My friend, thank you for this kind gesture, Adaobi is my daughter and I promise you that she is in good hands. Thank you once more. (*Adaobi and Emeka step out to dance. Suddenly Adaobi screams and goes limp. There is confusion as Adaobi is taken inside*).

Lights Out.

ANTIDOTE

Obi's compound. Obidia is being consoled by her friend Nnenna.

Nnenna:
It's alright now, don't kill yourself after all Adaobi is not dead.

Obidia:
Not dead you say? Does she look like a human being to you? With those beastly feet and hands. God where are you? My enemies will now mock me.

Nnenna:
Stop it Obidia, there is always a way out. After all, Odumnaka is with her.

Obidia:
I knew it, she is a witch. She bewitched my daughter. Am I the one that stopped her from having children of her own?

Nnenna:
But Adaobi asked that she should be brought. Moreover Obi is inside with them.

Obidia:
Nnenna the harm is already done, Odum wants to avenge her anger on me by killing my only child (*she sobs uncontrollably. Obi enters with Odum*).

Obidia:
How is she?

Obi:
Take it easy woman (*calls*). Nkume

Nkume:

Nna anyi
Obi:
Go to Nkwo's house with Odum. Tell him to announce to the villagers that everyone should follow Odum's instruction concerning the leaves she will give to them. Tell him that the survival of my only child, Adaobi depends on it.

Odum:
Thank you Nna anyi (*Odum exits with Nkume while Obidia stares in amazement*)

Obidia:
Nna anyi, do you know what you are doing?

Obi:
Please Nnenna, hurry, go with Odum. Collect some leaves for your household do as other do. (*Nnenna leaves stupefied*).

Obidia:
Please help me God. She has cast her evil spell on him too.

Obi:
Now Obidia, the cure to Adaobi's constant ailment is in Odum's leaves. And those leaves are on her husband's land.

Obidia:
You mean the market site.

Obi:
Yes. We will have to look for a new site. We judged her wrongly all along. Now, go in to Adaobi and…(*A piercing cry is heard from within. They both rush in*)

Lights out.

CLOSURE

Same setting, villagers gather in Obi's compound. Adaobi and Odum are present too.

Obi:
Once more, you are all welcome my people. I have summoned you all. Most of you may not know the reason for our gathering. I am also sure that most of you are wondering why Odumaka is here present. Adaobi, my daughter is here too perfectly okay.

Okonkwo:
Obi, I am sorry to interrupt you. I will ask that Odum excuse us for some
time. We are all aware of the laws of the land and they are binding on her

Uche:
I am in total support too. If not, I will leave. *(There is general consent)*

Obi:
Idichie, my people, if only you will, allow me to finish then you will understand the reason for her presence. I am more aware of the laws of the land than any of you because I am a custodian of tradition. Who made these laws? We did. Some of them are retrogressive, oppressive and selfish. Today there would be a waiver. Odum was never in the wrong. However, I have already directed that Owan proceeds with rites of appeasement to cleanse the land. To give you a clearer picture, I will allow Adaobi, my daughter to tell her story.

Adaobi:

(Comes forward and kneels down) Thank you papa. I greet everyone present here today. First, I have to ask for forgiveness from every one of you for this confession I'm about to make. Precisely three years ago, I went to the stream very early in the morning to fetch water for my mother in company of my friend Akunma. We were about filling our pots with water when suddenly we heard a strange noise. We both ran but I hit my leg against a stump and fell. Not long after, I felt a whirl wind hit me and that was all I remembered. I woke up to find myself at home being attended to by mother. I...

Obi:
Yes, go on my daughter

Adaobi:
Since then, from time to time, I would suddenly feel a force over whelming me from within and I wouldn't be able to stop it. Those are the periods I faint and remain unconscious for seven days. Whenever, I am in this state, I become an invisible beast with three heads and four eyes on each head. I travel to faraway places which I don't even know. On the seventh day, I will head back for my village. By then I would be famished by hunger. So, I eat up all plants, food and crops within my reach. This explains the constant devastation experienced in the village after the attack by the invisible beast. On the eight day I will wake up again as a normal human being.

(There are different reactions of surprise by villagers to this revelation)

Okonkwo:
Adaobi do you know what you are saying?

Udo:

You mean you are the one responsible for the destruction we have been experiencing?

Uche:

What of the death of our virgins?

Adaobi:

I myself cannot explain it. I don't know how it happens. I am not directly responsible. It was the evil force in me then.

Orji:

And now?

Adaobi:

Now I am free. All; thanks to our mother here Odumnaka. On my last journey, after my failed wedding I came to her husband barn on the seventh day as usual to eat up the yams but I perceived a strange odour which choked me up and rendered me inactive. When I woke up on the eight day, I was half human and half beast. I asked that she should be brought. I confided in her and my father and begged her to apply this same antidote all over the village.

Obi:

My people, Odum has helped our land despite our attitude to her *(there is silence)*. She has repaid our evil with good. Her insistence on not using her husband's land as the new market was because the leaves are on that land. Today she is here in our midst. How do we repay her for this kind gesture? *(There is a distraction from outside)*

Nkume:

(Rushes in) My Lord

Obi:

Nkume, what is it?

Nkume:
The young man you warned to stay away from... (Edozie runs in with torn clothes revealing his body)

Edozie:
I am the one my lord (*Adaobi runs to him but its prevented*)

Obi:
What do you want here again?

Old man:
I am his father. My name is Berumachu from Akagaa.

Obi:
Old man I have no business with you. As you are aware, I can do with you as I like. You are an enemy and you are in my territory.

Edozie:
I brought the cure for Adaobi's ailment (brings out some leaves. Everyone stares at him. Odum takes a closer look at the leaves)

Orji:
Get this mad boy out of here

Obi:
Nkume what are you waiting for?

Adaobi:
I will go with him (*goes to Edozie*)

Obi:
Are you out of your mind?

Adaobi:
Emeka has refused me as a bride and even your friend Igwe Akachi has annulled the marriage. You have returned my dowry to him. Papa this is the one my heart longs for

Obi:
An enemy?

Adaobi:
I love him Papa
Obi:
You will not have my blessing?
Odum:
(*Busy scrutinizing Edozie's body*). Obi, if you will permit me to intervene...
Obi:
You have no say in this matter, she is my daughter
Odum:
He is my son (*everyone looks at her in surprise*). Young man, how did you get these marks on your back?
Edozie:
My father says they're from birth
Odum:
And these? (*Pointing to the leaves in his hands*)
Edozie:
Oh, the leaves? I saw a woman in my dream. She...
Uche:
The boy is mad
Odum:
No. Go on my son
Edozie:
She showed me the leaves on my father's farm and asked me to bring it here
Odum:
This woman, what does she look like?
Edozie:

She's dark in complexion, two missing upper front teeth, plumb, has long grey hair…

Odum

Mama Nneoma. Today is a happy day for me, my people. God has answered my prayers. This is my son Ozoemena whom I lost several years back

Edozie:

Woman, you must be mistaken. I am not your son. My mother is dead and this is my father here. We are from Akagaa.

Odum:

Join me, my people, rejoice with me, my joy has come

Edozie:

Papa, let us leave at once

Old Man:

No, Edozie, my son, today you must know the whole truth today. I am not your biological father and Olanma did not give birth to you.

Edozie:

But papa...

Old man:

I know my son but you must know the truth. I found you in the bush twenty five years ago.

Odum:

Bush?

Old man:

Yes, I was hunting, you were there crying and all alone. I discovered that you had missed your way, I asked for your name but all you could say was mama. I searched round the bush but saw no one nor heard any sound. Since people from my village were forbidden from entering the village I couldn't bring you here. But I knew your parents would be from this village. Not willing to be killed, I took you home and gave you to my wife to nurse since she could not bear children. That is how you became our child.

Edozie:

But why? Why? Why? Papa?

Old man:

We were afraid that if you knew the truth all these years, you would return here. Forgive me my son.

Obi:

Odum how are you sure he is your lost son?

Odum:

Come, Edum, look at him closely. I had given birth to three healthy boys before him. The first died immediately after birth. The second waited until after the naming ceremony on the eight day. The third left same day he clocked a year. So when I had him we named him Ozoemenam. Some of you standing here were present at his naming. We were advised that to prevent him from going the way of others, we needed to inflict pains on him just like he had done to us severally. So, the Didia seared his back with three long marks using a hot knife. I cried daily as I nursed those wounds on his back for months. But I lost again when he was just a year and three months old. I took some clothes for washing at Abama River. One minute, he was beside me and the next he was gone while I was rinsing clothes in the river.

Edu:

I blamed her for her carelessness she shouldn't have allowed him to stray from her while washing. We inquired from the oracle and we were told that our son was alive and would walk back to us some day. After that my wife was never able to conceive again and she carries the guilt on her conscience like a heavy burden.

Odum:

I have waited long for this day

Edu:

Come Ozoeme, let me have a closer look at you

Edozie:

My name is Edozie not Ozoeme

Old man:

I gave you Chiedozie

Odum:

You are my Ozoemenam. My mother, the same woman you saw in your dream also gave me the leaves in your hands to end the attack of the invisible beast in our land. It is the antidote for Adaobi's constant. That is why we are all gathered today.

Edozie:

The leaves?

Odum:

Yes, this is it (*shows him the leaves with her*)

Old man:

Chiedozie go on, she is your mother. I have always known that a day like this would come

Odum:

This is your father

Dozie:

Mother... father... I... (*Odum and Edu embrace him*)

Old man:

My son persuaded me to come with him and speak with Obi concerning Adaobi

Obi:
The unfolding of events today have been like a dream. First I renounce all proclamations earlier made on Odum. From this moment she is one of us again. You are all free to associate with her as before (*there is jubilation*). Second, I welcome our lost son back home and rejoice with Chinedu and his wife (*cheers*).
Edum:
I have a request to make Nna anyi
Obi:
Go on
Edum:
I join my son Ozoeme to seek your consent for the hand of your beautiful daughter, Adaobi in marriage. I know this is not the right…
Obi:
That is a difficult request to make
Uche:
It seems today is a day of celebration, the gods are smiling on us today. I will implore that in the spirit of re-union, you consider this request, Obi. This young man is one of us, Odum's son. How else can we repay Odum for her many sacrifices for our land? Edozie also brought a cure for Adaobi risking his life. Please, my lord, be wise in your decisions. This is a perfect arrangement by the gods.
Odum:
Obi, I should be the one to refuse to give my consent. I suffered humiliation, reproach and shame just because of the love I have for my land. Yet when I was called upon in the time of need I stood for the village. And now, the truth has prevailed. Today I

am being reinstated and also reunited with my lost son. Obi, my joy will be complete if my son's request is granted.

Obi:

You have all spoken well, you all make me look like the tortoise who only wanted to take and take from others without giving in return. Adaobi, come here (*she kneels*). You have heard the request of this young man. What is your say on this?

Adaobi:

Papa, Dozie is the love of my life. I will marry him if you consent

Obi:

Dozie come over (*kneels*) I give my consent for you to marry Adaobi. Due process shall be followed for the marriage rites. Dozie you are welcome back home. Old man, thank you for taking care of our son. Today I declare free and friendly relationship between our land and your village Akagaa. I will also send the symbol of peace and friendship to your Obi on next Eke market. The wedding date shall be announced later when we shall all wine and dine.

Villagers:

Eeeeeee

Obi:

Finally, I decree that a festival will be held yearly starting from this year before the harvest, in remembrance of the sacrifices Odum made for our land. It shall be a festival of reconciliation, conflict resolution and peaceful co-existence among us and all neighbouring villages and towns. It shall be called Odum festival.

Oyinsi:

Obi, we thank you for this recognition given to one of us. Odum, although we did not believe in your cause but we are happy that you are victorious at the end.

Ijeoma:
My friend, please find a place in your heart to forgive us, your sisters and friends for letting you down when you needed us most.

Odum:
I hold no grudges against anyone. The battle was meant to be fought alone. But we will win many others together.

Orji:
Obi, I hope the men are safe. This one that our women are teaming up to fight battles?

Nkwo:
There's no need for battles. You will always take your rightful places beside us.

Odum:
Not only beside you. We will speak with one voice, act with one purpose and take our rightful place among great women of other climes.

Obi:
It gives me joy that our women are rising up to face challenges and also taking the lead in proffering solutions. You can count on our support at all times.

Oyinsi:
You Obi. Our father and leader with a difference. With your permission and in the spirit of jubilation, Umu Ada will do our special dance to celebrate Odum.

Nneoma:

No, I want to dance too. I've been back stage since. I want the audience to see me too. *(Other actors are angry for the disruption. Papa comes on stage)*

Papa:

It's alright, my children. We have come to the end of our story tonight. *(They all protest)*. Tomorrow is another day. My bones are weak and I need to sleep. Now, remove your costumes and clear this space. Your parents are waiting for you at home.

Ugo:

Papa, please let us have the last dance. Its celebration dance.

Children:

Please papa

Papa:

Okay, I give up. The last dance and we all go home. *(The children perform a well-choreographed dance which leads to curtain call). Lights out.*

The end

APOGEE (A suffragette fiasco)
Eziwho Emenike Azunwo

CHARACTERS

CHIEF ONUKWUARI - THE CHAIRMAN DUMBARIA MARKET
KINISOOME - VICE-CHAIRMAN
ESHISHI - MARKET LEADER
CHEARI - DEFENDER OF THE FEMALE FOLK
OKOSIMIEMA- FORMER MARKET PRESIDENT
MRS. ASHEL- FEMALE MEMBER
CHIEF PEACE- FEMALE
MS. ORUBEBE- SHADE OWNER
MR. MIEBI- A MAN
MR. NYO-UELOME – A MAN
MR. DERI-PADE – A MAN
MR. ISETIMA – A MAN
WOMEN
CROWD
NARRATOR

Drama One
SUBTERFUGE

The scene opens in an office decorated moderately to capture the essence of women. The atmosphere is chargely inflamed with high tension as songs of emancipation, liberation, solidarity and revolution chokes the background to a point of combustion. Suddenly, Merit gingered, instigated and even hypnotized the women more into action. To this effect, the women are spurred to react recklessly as if beaten by minors. The following characters are in attendance: Cheari, Eshishi, Okosimiema, Mrs. Ashley, Peace, and Ms Orubebe.

Okosimiema
Briefly (*clears her throat*) my dear friends and compatriots, welcome to this secret but emergency meeting of the meeting that will redefine our position as women in this our market. It is a redefining moment and I would love us to forge ahead together as an indivisible unit.

Cheari
Thank you, our leader and most politically conscious woman. Our future is here and we must strategise properly so that it will not sleep off from us.

Orubebe
And we must without delay commence so that Onukwuari will not meet us taking vital decisions concerning our future (*pauses and speaks further*) please I would like the convener of this August meeting to start swiftly so that we can dismiss and return to our various houses in time.

Okosimiema
Greatest market women!

All

Great!
Okosimiema
Greatest Dumbaria women
All
Great
Okosimiema
You're once again, welcome greatest and most successful market women of time. I have called all of you to explain to you that the future belongs to us and we must take it not only by force, but by stratagems!
Cheari
Speak on dear sister, the heavens will surely fall if we do not install our candidates and tumble this market for the good of mankind.
Ashley
The time has come for us to prove to the nation that the women have the best leadership materials this nation is in dire need of, and we must start showcasing it from the market.

Okosimiema
Greatest Dumbaria woman! Our task is a great one.

All
To keep the market clean
Okosimiema
Our task is a venerable type
All
To keep the market alive
Okosimiema
Our task is a godly one

All
To restore hope, dignity and pride to womanhood starting from the market.
Okosimiema
It is because of these and many other undisclosed reasons that we're meeting right here and now. We must assert ourselves to avoid hearing those stories that touch
All
O yes, we're and we must assert ourselves here and now completely.
Eshishi
(*Laughing frenziedly, suddenly speaks*) Now the male folks will know why they call us men with womb
All
(*Echo*) That's the power and composition of the women, and we are women, the nation builders.
Okosimiema
My fellow women, what we are doing here is a build-up meeting that will eventually launch us to the full manifestations of our womanhood. (*Simple pause*) we must remember that we have the key to the destiny of the world and must use them to our very advantage. (*Everyone claps and in laud whisper*) We are women and we must assert ourselves accordingly.
Peace
The world is at our finger tips and we must not let it slip from our hands. (*Looking at the women, then speaks further*) This is the opportunity we've long looked for and the world must hear our voices, yes, the voices of the women, even in the ultramodern market.

Okosimiema
Now to the reason why we've gathered together here. Our common goal which is....

All
To take over the leadership of the market from the men folks who over the years have wrongly forced themselves on the women by the help of tradition and culture.

Okosimiema
As educated women, we must work very hard in order to shift the paradigm for the betterment of the society. The paradigm shift must start with the forthcoming market election.

Cheari
We are ready for the paradigm shift and the shift must start with us today in this meeting.

Okosimiema
Talking about paradigm shift, you all know that we are still expecting Chief Onukwuari- the president of the Ultra-Modern Market of Dumbaria.

All
(Answer in affirmation) Yes

Okosimiema
(Smiles) Now that you know, how do we manipulate and sway him to our side?

Peace

Onukwuari is not a serious fellow that we should lose our sleep for!

Cheari

He is a cursed man and will be willing to betray any serious course if his emotion is fully satisfactorily engaged. Quote me!

Orubebe

(*Laughing*) Are you speaking from experience?

Cheari

Whatever, speak for yourself and leave me alone. He is a weak man whose emotions control the sense of his reasoning! Just promise to go down with him or supply him with some virgins. (*Smiles*) It will be case close and we have our way.

Okosimiema

Are you serious?

Cheari

You know you are always a very serious woman. (*Smiles*) He even said carelessly that he likes you and he would do anything to have you.

Orubebe

Case close!

Merit

Please stop the nonsense; I'm not interested in any fetid play! I'm a conscious woman who is always willing to defend the course of womanhood.

Cheari

Then do it and defend the womanhood, this is the best opportunity to help redefine our position in the society.

Merit

Over my dead body, I won't do it!

Cheari
You must do it once and for all, after all, you would agree to all his machinations and promise him once he sells out the male folks and push the power to the women, he would have all he needs, especially the daughters of eve!

Peace
Madam Merit, for your information, Onukwuari cannot resist anything in skirt. He will deny everything, sell the male folks and claim nobody slapped anyone. In fact, no meeting held.

Okosimiema
If it is that simple then it is a done deal. We must depart and prepare for Apogee, the Election Day. (*They embrace one another as they start departing from various exits. The scene fades out, overtaken by dark and music*)

Narrator
What is the meaning of this? What is this the women are saying about a man? And what is this fresh urgency about? Are they in any sort of revolution? So many what and what but then, I'm pretty sure these are the melodic rhythm pounding in the minds of many sitting in the audience right now. Well, to say by and large, the women have had it at their neck. They are tired of being pushed behind the fore by the men, they are tired of being placed in the background by dint of social stereotypes and patriarchy. Thus, they seek a change, they desire equality of between both sexes in both domestic and social concerns. (*A brief pause and a huge sigh*) ladies and gentlemen, this is a huge task and I'm pretty sure

none of us will be thinking otherwise (*Laughs*). Just to say the least friends and lovers of the theatre, as gigantic as this task seem to be, the women have decided to activate their insurrection from the market. This is a good fight, trust me. It's always interesting to fight for your right, nevertheless ladies and gentlemen, let's see how well these women will fight for theirs in this struggle of Apogee.

Drama Two
WOMEN ARE SAND

The scene opens in the office of the Market President. The office is properly arranged for the day's business. Officers present in the meeting include; the chairman (Chf. Onukwuari), the vice-chairman (Kinisoome) Female Market Leader, (Eshishi), and Cheari- a kind woman.

Onukwuari
(*The scene opens with great euphoria as the chairman addresses the people*). Yes, good morning ladies and gentleman).

All
Good morning, sir.

Onukwuari
(*Clears his throat and speaks further*) very soon, our market shall be engraved into Map of the world.

Eshishi
You say?

Onukwuari
What is the meaning of you say? Can't you listen attentively? Or are you deaf?

Cheari
(*Ugh! Eshishi and Cheari shock*) Presidooo please, do not address a responsible woman that way. You have just treated her like a skivvy and it is bad of you as the market president.

Onukwuari
(Tries to calm them) please forgive me, calm down. I will repeat myself, (*pauses*) even much more politely. It's like I wasn't loud enough......

Eshishi

Thank you for behaving like the gentle man that you are.

Onukwuari

Yes! Like I was saying, our market shall be on the world's map.

Cheari

Sir, that is very nice of you and I tell you, your effort shall not be in vain.

Eshishi

(*Laughs loudly and uncontrollably, pauses*) our President, I like you very much sir. And if I may ask, do you know why I like you?

Onukwuari

No madam (*looks at her with great surprise*)

Kinisoome

(*Stands and shouts*) Our unique market president, I am highly disappointed in you. Why should you apologize to her at all, an ordinary woman?

Onukwuari

Kinisoome, do you realize what you are doing? Do you realize you are the market, Vice President?

Eshishi

Please allow him to display his family attitude freely

Cheari

(*Laughs wisely*) He is showing his family face and you're busy preventing him!

Eshishi

(*Laughs and claps her hand*) Yes, that is what the fool is doing right here.

Onukwuari

(*Kinisoome still shouting*) Kinisoome, I say comport yourself and be reasonable else, you will lose your position accordingly.

Eshishi
What examples will this fellow show to the non EXECOS? It is bad of him, I must confess.
Cheari
Let's forgive him and forget his attitude, who knows whether it is only a carryover from his youth? Very soon, he shall grow and get matured in the mind (*laughs*)
Onukwuari
Is it in the grave?
All
Laugh (*Kinisoome sits down*)
Kinisoome
I promise I will not repeat it at all, I mean, I will not repeat it again
Eshishi
Mr. Man, there is need to hear from the women. Women have a lot to offer.
Cheari
That's true my sister
Onukwuari
Chief. Kinisoome, thank God you are returning to your senses, even urgently. May I quickly warn you for the last time? In no way must you repeat this act of buffoonery. (*Shouts from all directions*) I think you are not a buffoon or a nincompoop. I hope I have made myself vividly clear to you?
Kinisoome
Buffoonery? That isn't polite though! I am promising again that I shall not repeat it, you've addressed yourself like a clown acting in the theatre. This is indeed painful. But...
Onukwuari

(*Cuts in*) painful you mean? See… you better don't repeat it again!

Kinisoome

Okay sir. Where were we before we went on the dramatic break?

Cheari

At the point of engraving your Ultra-Modern Market, my Ultramodern Market, your Ultramodern Market and our own Ultra-Modern Market. That is, engraving the Ultra-Modern Market of Dumbaria into world's map.

Eshishi

Presido, before the dramatic display sir, that was exactly where we were.

Onukwuari

Then, we are right in order

Kinisoome

Exactly sir, we are…

Eshishi

(*Laughs*) He has started again

Cheari

No, he is just getting composed again.

Kinisoome

That's true

Onukwuari

Okay, fellow market people, I am repeating myself. The Ultra-Modern Market of Dumbaria shall be engraved into the world's map (*everybody claps*)

Eshishi

(*In shock and manages to ask a question*) How do you mean sir?

Onukwuari

You all know that my tenure as the president of this great Ultra-Modern Market of Dumbaria is elapsing soonest.

All
Yes, we are aware

Eshishi
Sir, not just yourself alone but, also the tenure of all your EXCOS

Kinisoome
(*Kinisoome speaks to the people*) Our tenure is elapsing and soon we shall be handing over to the next set of officers to man the affairs of this great market.

Cheari
That's true, Kinisoome has started his logicality again (*mass laughter*)

Onukwuari
It is my pleasure to announce to you that I won't be renewing my tenure in this our Ultra-Modern Market, because of greater responsibility ahead of me.

Kinisoome
(Stands to prostrate) Sir, I am happy for you. Please, receive my congratulations. It is another avenue for growth and mentorship for this great Ultra-Modern Market. (Smiles) I hear his Excellency the Executive Governor is considering him for an appointment.

Eshishi
God has answered our prayers again, and our connection is now stronger even in government. We can now stand bold and talk like those with political connections.

Cheari

We thank the Lord for this miracle. It is a thing of joy, and we have to celebrate at once.

Onukuari

Yes, celebration is secondary and shall come up thereafter. We shall continue with the crucial matter and later go to the frolicsome ones

Kinisoome

(*Cuts in with exclamation*) Ayaya! Which are the crucial matters that shall come before our celebrations? Listen, celebration is a thing of joy and it's contagious too! We shall go ahead and celebrate; I am ready to sponsor that session.

Cheari

Chf. please, don't take us back to another dramatic irony, let's consider the crucial matters first and after………

Kinisoome

(*Cuts in again*) Have you known the crucial matters? In fact, as for me, the most crucial matter is the celebration of his appointment.

Eshishi

I think it is wise for us to wait and hear the crucial matter from our outgoing president.

All

Laugh and applaud

Onukwuari

Thank you all! I must thank you all for listening and giving me all the supports at the crucial moments of my administration

Cheari

What are friends for? We succeed by helping one another and we shall continue supporting each other until our Ultra-Modern Market gets to the state of apogee (everybody applaud)

Onukwuari

Now, to the most crucial matter (*everybody smiles*). My tenure ends next week and I shall resume duty next month end as an appointee of the state governor. And the matters on the table now are, who are the most qualified persons to man the vacant position? Even Chf. Kinisoome has shown us that he is neither fit for the position nor…

Kinisome

(*Cuts in*) Presido., I think we have settled this problem of fitness long ago? Please, let's go ahead and discuss this crucial matter at length

Cheari

I think he is right sir, let's consider it right away

Eshishi

My ear is itching to hear more on this crucial matter

Onukwuari

My fundamental reason for calling this meeting (*pauses*), you all are special, and I think you can advise me accordingly.

Cheari

It is sine qua non for us to know how we can be of help to you right now sir.

Onukwuari

(*Smiles*) Yes, my people, most times, I wonder how many graduates have turned to market men and women in this our great market. I want us to reason together and select those people with great credibility to man the various offices.

Eshishi

Now you have come out boldly and thoroughly too. I will like to say that all the positions are major and must all be contested!

Kinisoome
What are you insinuating woman?
Onukwuari
(*Moves suddenly*) My people, you have to take things easy. All we need to do now is to think and nominate those persons who are qualified for the various positions
Cheari
I think Chf. Kinisoome should make his nominations first and after him, Eshishi, then I and if necessary, you Chf. Onukwuari either nominate or advises us

Kinsoome
Thank you Cheari for thinking like a mother and for giving me the position in the society, for even the HOLY BIBLE tells us that the man is always the head of the house
Eshishi
My friend, I do not know what is in your mind, but I think God has touched you and you have started vomiting them, one after another
Onukwuari
Please, we are not here to wash our dirty linen. Let's swallow everything that has brought misunderstanding in the past
Cheari
Are we still going through all that again? Time is no longer on our side. Please our people; let's hurry so as to leave on time, for we are all aware that the town is bad these days
Onukwuari
Let's stop beating about the bush and go straight to the point of our discussion

Kinisoome
Okay sir, I am nominating the following persons. Chf. Kinisoome for the position of the Ultra-Modern Market of Dumbaria President, Agog Ame gets General Sec, Johnson gets Financial Sec...

Eshishi
(*Cuts in*) Must you stop all these blabbing and allow a reasonable fellow to say something

Kinisoome
Who is the reasonable fellow? You or who? Listen let me address you properly, in case you do not know yourself. You are only a crone from Egypt

Cheari
Jesus! Enough of this your insult and swaggering of your tongue. Please listen carefully, this should be the very last time you will raise your voice rudely against any woman in my presence...

Kinisoome
(*Cuts in*) Madam, sit down and understand that you are very senile.

Onukwuari
(*Stands to calm the situation*) Kinisoome!! Kinisoome! Kinisoome!!! No response? How many times did I call you?

Kinisoome
Sir, three times sir...

Onukwuari
Enough of the ranting and raving. What is the matter with you all? Do you not realize that everybody would be famous for fifteen minutes?

Kinisoome
(*Stands to speak*) Sir it ...
Onukwuari
My friend, sit down and shut your mouth. Don't you know that businessmen achieving oneness will move on to "twoness"? Please Eshishi, I apologize on his behalf. You can go on with your nomination.
Cheari
Yes, my sister, ignore every attempt to distract you from nominating those people with trustworthy qualities.
Onukwuari
Eshishi, please get us their names and the most likely positions
Eshishi
I nominate Mrs Merit Ultra-Modern for Market President, Mrs. Joy for Gen Sec., Mrs. Ashley for Financial Sec., Mrs. Peace for Treasurer, others can be shared between females and males. (*The men are shocked*)
Kinisoome
Enough of the sentimental claptrap, enough of the calumny! Enough of the clangour, enough I say, enough of...
Onukwuari
Kinisoome, try and comport yourself. Remember you promised helping us that we will decide the fate of this great Ultra-Modern Market of Dumbaria (*Kinisoome rises to beg*). Chf. please, do not say that to her again
Kinisoome
I am very sorry, but you will understand my point soon (claps his hands and looks at them)

Cheari
Please continue my fellow women, for the floor is all yours.
Eshishi
Thank you, my sister, like I was saying…
Onukwuari
Enough madam! What are we actually doing here? Are we just displaying as puns? I am highly flabbergasted in this meeting
Kinisoome
I am equally staggered and astonished…
Eshishi
Why not die instead?
Onukwuari
(*Cuts in*) why mention dubious elements with questionable characters?
Cheari
Pardon? Who are those with dubious characters, the male or the female?

Onukwuari
There is no point engaging in meaningless arguments or in fabricating meaningless *meaninquities*! I think my position right now is still influential in this matter
Kinisoome
Yes, sir! Please do something before the situation goes out of hand
Eshishi
We urge you to say something and save your firing dart
Cheari

What are you waiting for? Please, say something. It is the most crucial moment; I say emphatically say something!

Onukwuari

Since you have over demanded and over pressurized me, I will certainly say something and it must be very shocking to some people

Eshishi

What are you waiting for? Our ears are itching. We want to hear what you have for us.

Onukwuari

Well, I have weighed all the nominations. I want to say that the nomination is not balanced. Kinisoome's viewpoint is partially okay, but I need a woman for the position of the Ass. Gen Sec…

Kinisoome

Sir, it shall be looked into analytically and critically

Onukwuari

Like I was saying before Kinisoome interrupted. Eshishi's nomination, I cannot stomach those women, they are dubious

Eshishi

(*Stands sharply*) What? Who are…

Cheari

(*Cuts in*) Fellow wemen, wait, he is just floating, just allow him to land first and after that, we can here and now respond effectively

Kinisoome

(*Smiles at them*) The secret mystery is getting unfolding

Eshishi

(*Whispers to Cheari*) Listen, I don't think I can still control my anger, the blood boils, the mouth foams and I'm...

Cheari
My sister wait, do not prompt them, just allow them and we shall react almost simultaneously....

Eshishi
Okay! That's okay by me

Onukwuari
You know some of the women that Cheari and Eshish nominated are dubious crooks

Eshishi
What? Am I not clear yet?

Kinisoome
Hear him clearly, he has started landing

Onukwuari
I shall not allow them hold any position in this institution

Cheari
I hope you have "okayed" my nomination?

Onukwuari
Who said that? I am still going through the names because some of them are much stained. Henceforth, I will never allow women hold any position

Eshishi
Mr. President or what are you called? I hope you are not sent to torment the female folk in this market? And...

Kinisoome
(*Cuts in at once*) Madam, you may better chew your word before they are released. You may even conclude that this continuous

struggle for female emancipation has toppled the whole market leadership. All I know is that his decisions bind us all. After all, he should have a successor plan!

Cheari

God forbid! I forbid! She forbids! We the entire female folk forbid it a long time ago.

Onukwuari

(*Still nodding*) Go ahead, that's a good display of intellectualism. It…

Eshishi

(*Cuts in sharply*) intellectualism? What is this foolish man saying? A man who does not know his left from his right.

Cheari

(*Laughs*) Eshishi, please take it easy

Eshishi

Take what easy?

Onukwuari

My decisions must bind on you all. No woman would hold any position in this market and that is final

Cheari

That is not possible!

Eshishi

Over my dead body! That cannot be final

Onukwuari

Who said that?

Eshishi

Over my dead body! Enough of that…

Onukwuari

Women shall not hold any position again in this market because they are not fit

Cheari
What? Why? How do you mean?

Onukwuari
Women shall not hold any further positions in this market because they are dust (*women are shocked*)

Kinisoome
Sir, please say it again

Onukwuari
(*Smiles*) Nothing dey happen. Women are not just dust alone, women are sand. Sand which we hoof upon. Women are sand, I say they're mere sand!

Eshishi
What? (*Moves closer to Onukwuari*)

Onukwuari
Women are SAND (*spells it in capital letters*). They are sand. In fact, they are sandy soil in this market.

Eshishi
(*Slaps him twice on his face*) God punish you a million times. Fool.

Kinisoome
(*Tries to move*) What? What have you just done? Why must a woman be this violent?

Cheari
(*Seats him down, slaps him and spits on his face*) Fool! Must you always show your family face?

Eshishi

This is an example of what an educated woman hates. Don't these men know that? (Attempts pointing finger at them) this is a woman's world and we mustn't allow you rubbish us here too!
Cheari
I hope they've learnt their lessons?
Onukwuari
(*Rises from his seat*) Am I dreaming? Is this a reality or an allusion that a woman, a lesser being to have slapped me? (*Shouts*)
Eshishi
It is not an illusion; it is real and very natural too. I think that serves you best and if care isn't taken, I'll repeat it.
Kinisoome
So, you are still talking and boasting all over in this meeting? We will deal with all of you.
Cheari
There is nothing any of you can do, except you want to lose your lock-up shops!
Onukwuari
You dare slap me? (Pauses amidst a seldom silence) how can a woman fearlessly met out violence on an older man with superior authority?
Eshishi
Let him arrogate authority to himself, that women, God's own gift to humanity are sand!
Cheari
Presido you should be thankful to God Almighty that I woke up today from the right side of the bed
Onukwuari

(*Stands*) My sledged hammer has seen whom to fall upon this season (*walks out of the stage angrily*)

Eshishi

Cheari, please come let's leave immediately before something more dramatic happens to us (*the women hurry out of his office*)

Kinisooome

Now, I am left alone in president's office to do what? I don't know, should I take his place as the Presido? What have we been doing? Holding or hosting talk? Are women really sand? Or are the men confused? I think (*pause*). These questions shall all be answered soon at the emergency meeting (*but during the above speech, the play fades out and is overtaken by dark and music*)

Drama Three
MEN ARE CONFUSED

This scene opens in Ashley's office, the market secretary. The office is beautifully arranged to reflect her position. The wall is decorated with the pictures of the president of the nation and the governor of the state, wall clock, calendar, university gown, convocation pictures of Ashley, a set of pictures showing her husband, children and herself and the framed picture of holy Mary, the mother of God. The office is quite large, containing a telephone, assorted books, files, a pack of pen and sheets of paper. Present among the female include; Cheari dressed on black gown and white bandana with a pair of medicated glasses, Eshishi dressed on black skirt suit, Mrs. Ashley dressed on white trouser suit, Dr. Peace, dressed on black jeans trouser and yellow T-shirt, Okosimiema, dressed on azure blue trouser suit, Ms Orubebe, dressed on off colour jean trouser and T-shirt to match.

Cheari
(*Rises to greet her fellow comrades with great enthusiasm and famous delight as she empties her mind and system*) Good day fellow comrades and people of courage

All
(*Responds*) Good day wise one and the defender of womanhood

Cheari
Thank you very much. I am so glad that you have started understanding why I called for this rendezvous and why I chose this place as the venue

Eshishi
Every reasonable woman should, I suppose

Ashley
I think we are clear on that and do not need much greetings and commendations

All
That's true
Cheari
My people, I have invited you here to let you know how low we are in the eyes of men of this great market "Ultra-Modern Market of Dumbaria"
Okosimiema
You mean.... We are low, down trodden, unheeded and considered as nothing?
Eshishi:
Exactly! You are very correct, my sister and strong colleague in the business of struggle for womanhood
Okosimiema
You don't mean it (*shocked*)
Cheari
It is no longer news that the men, I mean.... Those who view us from the ear (she demonstrates with her hand) and call us motor, have been planning evil against us
Orubebe
Motor! What does that mean?
All
(*Laugh...... hahahahahahahahaha*) You must be a total stranger in this market!
Orubebe
(*Surprise*) Oh! You are all laughing at me, comrade (*she nods her head, wipes her face with a handkerchief*)
Cheari
President, my president, our own president, preziidoooo! (*She hails her*)

All
Preziidooo, nothing spoil, we are in order.
Orubebe
(Smiles and reacts to the hailing) Thank you my people. The problem is that of misunderstanding. I misunderstood the whole issue
Eshishi
That's why we are here in order to iron out issues and give clear meaning where necessary
Cheari
Thank God we are together. Lest I forget, where were we before now?
All
We were knocked down by the motor the male folk call us
Cheari
Motor, my dear, they look at our asses, call us motor and classify us all.
Orubebe
What do you mean? Please give us the various classifications

Cheari
My dear, your size determines the type of motor you are
Okosimiema
How do you mean?
Cheari
My dear, some are called Mercedes Benz V-Boot. They call some of us 190,230,500 series, etc.
They even call some Toyota Spider, Big for nothing, Pickup, Tipper, Golf, Padded, Volvo, Passat and even Okada.

All

(*Laugh and shout*) Okada too!!!

Cheari

Are you kidding me? Thank God peace has finally returned to our camp and we must go ahead discussing our aim for gathering

Eshishi

Well, we thank the Lord our God

Peace

Men! Men! Men! We shall show you our true colour now and I mean it

Cheari

I like that spirit. It is the spirit of togetherness.

Peace

The time has come for us to show them why God almighty chose to make women

All

The time has really come and we shall show them that we are ready

Cheari

(*Smiles and speaks further*) women, radicals, leftists and great women. I like being in the top of the whole wide world. I mean, I am happy, challenged and charged. We shall together upgrade our female folk in this market.

All

We are solidly behind you. You have our support and mandate, carry-on

Cheari

Those illogical elements opened their abscessed mouths and cursed us. I promise with determination they shall reap the fruit of their lips. I promise them!

Okosimiema

My fellow women, I am highly disappointed at those men.

Eshishi

They called us names and equated us to some filthy elements.

Cheari

Please calm down. I am presiding over this rendezvous meeting and I shall deliver on our mandate accordingly. I am in charge here.

Eshishi

Okay, I agree with you. No confusion! No problem! We are together

Okosimiema

Please Cheari, go ahead and preside, we shall decide

Eshishi

(*Emphatically*) we shall decide and you shall preside

Cheari

(*Resumes again and talks to the women*) Those idiots called us names (*pauses*) Yes, they called us names!

Okosimiema

My ears are itching for the news. I need the news even now

Cheari

The young man told us in the meeting that his tenure as the president of the Ultra-Modern Market of Dumbaria has just ended

Eshishi

And the tenure of every other officer in the market

Cheari

Yes! Their tenure has just ended and he told us the need for a new leadership and gave us the opportunity to make nominations…Yes, we made some nominations…

Eshishi

That's not all. So many things were basically trashed in the meeting

Peace

What did they actually trash?

Cheari

Fellow women, Eshishi's nominees, they regarded them as null and void. And they said women were dubious elements

Eshishi

(*Cuts in*) It is true. I mean, I was thoroughly disgraced just because I nominated some women to man the various advertised positions (*shakes her head*). The world must surely hear this and justify us

Cheari

My people, my own nominations were also disregarded.

All

What? (*Snap their fingers over their head*) Kai! Chei! God forbid!

Cheari

Yes, God has already forbidden it long-long time ago. (*Low whisper*) Listen, my people, death I think is already standing above those men. I know not what has gone into their ears… of their strange language. All I know is that there is a word of fear in their lives

Merit

(*Looks around nodding her head*) Time shall surely tell

Eshishi
May God Almighty deliver us from the trap of those men
All
Amen
Eshishi
Women should make themselves to be respected by men, less their place be denied by the men of this market and society at large
All
Supported!!
Ashley
Those people who call themselves male chauvinists are unscrupulous and violent
Okosimiema
How on earth will they reason like that? Those men (*pauses*) are they actually humans?
All
Yes! Human beings indeed!
Cheari
To be more precise said: "Women shall not hold any position in this market again because they are not fit" …
Okosimiema
(*Shocked*) They are not fit?
Eshishi
Just listen attentively because she has not said all
Okosimiema
This is unbelievable!
Cheari
He further stated that "we are DUST"

All
(*Shouting in one voice*) Why this evil?
Okosimiema
You don't mean it! God! We are finished. What ridicule (*All the women are shocked*)
Cheari
He boldly said "nothing dey happen, women are not only dust, they are sand" (*reaction from all the women*).
Okosimiema
(*Stands and speaks in punctuating voice*) This is highly disheartening. What did you people do?

Eshishi
My sister, listen, I slapped him, I mean the president, twice on his face. He cried and called it a "Bazooka slap"
Ashley
That's good, it is an introduction to what we shall be doing to them
Cheari
I equally slapped Kinisoome twice on his face.
Peace
That is too bad as an educated woman
Eshishi
(Pauses) Stop that at once. Why should you speak evil from your mouth?
Peace
Well, I have spoken. I do not think slapping or beating up men means women emancipation. Let us try and apply dialogue and tactical diplomacy.

Orubebe
(*Laughs*) Diplomacy indeed!
Ashley
Please women, let's give them ten gbosas
All
(*Exactly*) Gbosa! Gbosa! Gbosa!
Okosimiema
What was their reaction?
Cheari
You should trust our president he cried and started talking without control

Some Women
(*Laugh*) Ha hahahaha aha ha
Ashley
This is funny. That is what the theatre people call drama
Okosimiema
What was Kinisoome's reaction? That bad and proud man
Eshishi
He talked of calling emergency meeting
Peace
Let's put our house together before the male folk take us by surprise and scatter us. Listen, anyone who is not shocked by female decision has not understood it yet
Okosimiema
You are not just thinking, but you are being logical
Ashley
That's true. Your mind is working perfectly well
Cheari

I want us to know that the reverse side also has a reverse side. It is intelligence and nothing else that has to be opposed. What do we do? Yes, the slap. I suggest that we send some of our wicked friends to caution them before hand, least our position as women in this market will be made vulnerable.

Okosimiema
You did not slap anybody!
Cheari
(*Surprises*) How do you mean?
Okosimiema
Did you slap anybody? The answer is capital NO. Was the meeting recorded by anyone?
Cheari
None
Okosimiema
Was any minute taken?
Eshishi
No
Okosimiema
Then you don't have any problem. In fact, that day, at exact that hour, I will say we were with the community women leader ironing out some issues concerning our association
Cheari
Merit, in fact, your wisdom demands that you be the next president of this great market. Please, let us give our new president a standing ovation (*all stand and clap*). Let's take our seats
Peace
This is not good enough. Let's give her ten gbosa

All
Gbosa! Gbosa! Gbosa!
Peace
Let us give the clown Ekaite
All
Ekaite…
Cheari
I think we have come to the apogee of the rendezvous. Does anybody still have anything more to say? (Hands raise from all directions)
Eshishi
Let us keep this decision to ourselves
Cheari
That is very important
Okosimiema
We shall take an oath to be very sure
Cheari
That's the best option. What are we still waiting for? Let's do it! (*it raises mixed reactions among the women. Upon a moment of brief silence, Merit gets a cup filled with drink, holds hands together with other women, mutters some words and chants, sips from the cup and passes to other women*).
Cheari
My people, those men do not realize that the world is ruled by letting things take their course, but they rather keep disturbing the cause of nature thereby creating disequilibrium everywhere.

Eshishi
Fellow women, may I delay you a little with few questions

Okosimiema
Common! Carry on! We want to listen and learn more from you
Eshishi
Thank you very much! Please, can someone tell me why a woman's place in the public has been so restricted? Is a woman an inferior creation of God, destined for subordination in her family, marketplace, community and world at large? (*No reply*)
Eshishi
Does the redemption of Christ include both women are men? Or is it limited according to gender?
Cheari
The audience is listening. Let the audience answer!
Orubebe
Since Eve first partook of the forbidden fruit, are women justified before and through Christ from all sins-except that one?
Cheari
The priest can't even answer this question (*laughing*)
Ashley
My own question to the men is quite simple. Is justification from all sins only available to men alone?
Cheari
(*Looks at her and shakes her head*) A man without a woman is a paralyzed spirit in dirt walking on two legs. We shall take a break, when we return these and many more questions shall be posed to the men in the meeting and if they are unable to provide answers to them, we shall declare them confused (*They embrace one another as they start departing from various exits. but during the speech and prayer, the play fades out, overtaken by dark and music*)

Drama Four
DRAMA FOUR
APOGEE

The scene opens in the president's office. The hall is highly decorated to match the meeting taking place in it. Prominent among characters in the meeting include: Onukwuari- the president of the Ultra-Modern Market of Dumbaria, *dressed in black suit. Kinisoome- the vice president, Cheari, Eshishi, Okosimiema , Mrs. Ashley, Peace, Ms Orubebe, Mr. Miebi, Mr.Nyo-ite, Mr.Peri-pade and Mr.Isetima. The president walks in, everyone stands, he takes a bow and sits, everyone also bows and sits. Onukwuari bows and sit. Amongst the people, their random murmuring regarding the recent happening in town.*

Onukwuari

(*Immediately takes over the full moderation of the meeting*). People, your complaints have been noted. Immediate action will be taken to resolve the issue (*they smile with great hope and expectation*)

Cheari

Speedily

Onukwuari

We shall leave on time, if every comrade focuses more attention on the issue on ground. I do not want this meeting to drag till evening

Cheari

I think that is good for us all

Onukwuari

And to start with the business of the day, the agenda are as follows (*Eshishi nods her head and winks her eyes to some active female stakeholders as soon as the issue of the election of the new president is mentioned)*

Onukwuari
To start the ball rolling, I want to thank you all for coming for today's meeting. I promise that at the end of the day, we shall all know why we are here and where we heading!

Ashley
Sir, I think we have danced enough for the day. Please, let's get to the business of the day. We have about fifteen items to discuss. Let's get started at once because you already know where my mind is…

Orubebe
(Cuts in) And where else could your mind be except for the election of the new president and other EXCOS? *(The women laugh)*

Cheari
That's the main reason why we are here. Let's see how we can unanimously move our institution forward

Uyo-Uelome
(Reacts sharply) Let's stop beating about the bush. Let's forge ahead to tie-up the untied knobs and allow the chairman to preside over this meeting.

Onukwuari
Yes, I think we are going backward in this meeting. I want us to avoid every discussion that will make us loss focus on today's business. *(Discussing with registrar in aside and later resumes his speech).* Agenda number two is very crucial, I think.

Orubebe
(Laughs) The most crucial!

All
Oh yes! The most crucial of them all
Orubebe
Well, if it's the most crucial, having taken care of the first item in the agenda, let's kick the ball rolling.
Miebi
Supported
Onukwuari
That's okay. The second agenda is who are the people to succeed the present officers whose tenure has expired. (*Looks around and nods his head gently*). (*Looks at Kinisoome*) Would like your sir, to withdraw that statement at once
Miebi
My dear, I hope you have not decided to rain insult on me and other women here?
Kinisoome
Please do not cause a total breakdown of law and order here.
Nye-Uelome
What are you doing Kinisoome? (*There is a little misunderstanding among the excos and the president intervenes*)
Onukwuari
People, please calm down, so that we can effectively handle the business of the day, which is the election of the president.
Kinisoome
If that be the case, I am happy with the development. (*Turns to the president, smiles and resumes his speech*). Sir, time has come for us to revenge the slap that was issued to us during our last meeting
Eshishi

(*Cuts in*) Who slapped who? When? Why? (*Eshishi and Cheari look at each other with a special signal*)

Onukwuari

(*Clears his throat and response*) My people, I don't understand what the young man is saying. I think it will be proper for us to give him an opportunity to explain. I am amazed at the revelation. (*On aside*) What does this man want to say? (*Turns to Kinisoome*) you can tell the house what you have in mind

Kinisoome

(*Stands, clears his voice and speaks*) Wonders shall never cease. It's a wonder not to acknowledge wonderful deeds. Yes, I should say it because you have just denied the slap you called "Bazooka slap"

...

Onukwuari

(*Cuts in*) My dear, I wasn't slapped by anybody (*emphatically*). Kinisoome, let me make it abundantly clear to you and to everyone here. I am a proud prince and the royal blood flows in my vein. Therefore, no man born of a woman can lift his hand against me and not drop dead. (*The women look at each other with great surprise*). Better still, maybe you were slapped in the dream world. I have not held any meeting with anybody since I was recently appointed. Maybe you should take some malaria drugs

Eshishi

(*Breaks in, points at Kinisoome*) I think this man is sick. (*Looks at the women*)

All the Women

Yes! This man is sick

Eshishi

Can you recall how many times he has disrupted our meeting today? It is obvious that Kinisoome is suffering from classical hallucination. If not for the respect I have for the men and constituted authority, I would have raised a motion for his immediate suspension and …

Ashley

Madam, please that is not what we have come here for

Eshishi

(*Angrily*) This man has forged his story and he is very proud of it. I think he did it out of hate for the president.

Kinisoome

(*With great surprise*) What is happening?

Onukwuari

(*Innocently cuts in*). Enough of the sentimental claptrap. I say enough! We must be thinking of how to uphold peace

Miebi

Yes. Peace option is what we need

Kinissome

(*Still in shock*) Well, if that is the case, let me join the peace option. (*Surprising everybody with his words, he continues*). That was acted like mere drama. Cheari slapped and spat on me, while Eshishi slapped the presido twice. Well, if it's a dream, let it be. All I know is that either the president has been bribed or he is ashamed of what people will say. He shall receive much more slap and beating in his life from the women

Onukwuari

Let's get back to more pressing issues

Nye-Uelome

(*Laughing*) If there was no slap at all, either directly or indirectly, let us continue, but if there was, let's set up a committee to look into it at once

Cheari

Supported! I am strongly in support

Onukwuari

EXCOS, we have passed that level. I am boldly saying that we have come to the state of Apogee, I mean, the state of decision

All

Yes. The state of Apogee

Onukwuari

Without further delay, let's go straight to the appointment and election of the officers respectively. Those who will man the various offices for the next tenure

Orubebe

This is Apogee

Deri-Pade

(*Smiles*) That is the seat of decision making.

All

Yes!

Kinisoome

Apogee, yes! But let it be done with caution! (*The women put their heads together and whisper to one another. They at once start circulating fliers, seeking the support of the senators in the election of the position of the president*)

Onokwuari

My people, we have truly come to the state of Apogee, the state which everybody has been waiting for. (*Suddenly, a host of market women un-invitedly burst into the scene in a manner of protest, singing and chatting in enthusiasm*).

Kinisoome

Who are these hoodlums!!! Who hired them to distract our proceedings? Can you all leave this place already? Who told you, you are fit to have a place in such a serious gathering as this? (*The already charged protesters are reluctant to leave*)

Onukwuari

Kinisoome, don't be too forward. At least I'm still here as your leader to make critical decisions.

Kinisoome

I'm sorry Mr. Chairman

Onukwuari

That's OK (*to the protesters*) why are you here?

A Protester

We are here to support the appointment and inauguration of our new market leader. (*To the other women*) Abi no be so?

All

Na So ooo!!!

Onukwuari

But.... (*Cuts in*)

Eshishi

Able chairman, please let them be. Afterall, they are as we are critical stakeholders in this great market. Let them at least grace the inauguration of their new market leaders.

Onukwuari

Ok. I share in your opinion. (*To the protesters*) Please settle in. So where were we before?

Eshishi

The very stage we have been waiting for! (*The women are seen seriously making some diplomatic moves with their eyes, as well as passing notes to the male senators*)

All

(*In Unison*) Apogee!!!

Onukwuari

Comrades, please remember that the executives' election is always a secret ballot system and I would ask that we please vote according to our conscience

All

(*Responding together*) Yes, conscience is an open wound only the truth can heal.

Onukwuari

(*Speaks further*) For the position of the President, we have Merit and Isetima. Please note that the election result shall be announced immediately.

All

We are all together. (*Ballot papers are being distributed to the comrades. The election is being conducted in a free and fair manner and the result is immediately being announced*)

Onukwuari

Ladies and gentlemen, Merit has won the day. (*There is a great jubilation. He continues calling other results and the women won almost all the positions except that of vice president and Ass Sec Gen., while Miebi and Isetima were elected respectively*)

Ashley

(*With excitement*) My people, they say the journey of one thousand miles begins with just a step. It is obvious that this market will be taking a new look. I pray for God's guidance upon us all, especially our new president, Merit

All

Amen

Onukwuari

Having conducted a new election/selection, we now have a new President who happens to be the former Sec. Gen. in the person of Merit. Please, let her come up and take her proper seat.

(*Everyone claps as Merit and Onukwuari exchange their sitting positions*)

Okosimiema

(*Smiles*) I want to express my profound gratitude to every one of you who in no little measure have contributed to my elevation to the position of the president. Onukwuari and all the women of this great ultra market, I promise that we shall all smile. To the women folk, remember I am your servant

Peace

Amen

Orubebe

(*Speaks to Merit*) Yes, I have contributed so much, especially in words. My unreserved contribution is what I will offer

Okosimiema

Thank you, my president, women with less words but more action, great women of value.

All Women

President! The great woman of value.

Orubebe

I still have more things to say…
Deri-Pade
(*Cuts in*) Orubebe, why can't you postpone the gossip till you get to your women's meeting?
Merit
Deri-Pade, listen, I do not want to get the impression that you are outmoded
Onukwuari
(*Looks at Merit*) What are you saying to a complete man?

Okosimiema
My friend shut up your mouth and sit down. I can't remember talking to you
All The Men
(*Shock*) Is this how she is going to rule us?
Eshishi
That is just a tip of the iceberg

Onukwuari
(*Clears his throat*) Well, as the new minister of…, I will use my position to retire you without your benefits
Kinisoome
That's just the beginning
Okosimiema
Yes, just the beginning of a new dawn. (*Calls*) Orubebe!
Orubebe
Yes, president.
Okosimiema

Bring that letter and read it to the house (*She brings the letter and reads it to the hearing of the excos*). That letter is from the presidency. As you have heard, Onukwuari's tenure has ended

Orubebe
"Dear, Mr Onukwuari, letter of termination…"

Kinisoome
My presido, why?

Okosimiema
Based on his inability to control his temper and thereafter slapping a woman twice in a meeting he will do worst things if he's elected.

Kinisoome
(*Laughs and turns to Onukwuari*) This is just the beginning. Please prepare for more surprises from your friend

Okosimiema
(*Stands to address the people*) I want to thank you all for actually giving me the opportunity to preside over this meeting. I promise not to disappoint you. Once again, I say a very big thank to all of you! (*Merriment in the air, especially amongst the women for their victory, all of a sudden, one of the women amongst the protesters raises a tough caution*)

Women
Nooooooooooooooooooooo…. (*Silence every as all attention shifts towards her direction*) Come to think of it compatriots, should we comfortably accepts undemocratic elements such as; excessive manipulation, blackmail, foul play, intrigue and ghykhanism? Eshishi NO! You are fraudulent!!

Eshishi
What is wrong with you? Or are you sent down from hades to occasion maximum catastrophic disaster here?

Woman

The fight for gender equality is not a war against the men and the society. If women must be emancipated fairly and truly from stigmatization of all strata then, we must come to terms with moderation, lawful enterprise and justice (*Brief pause*). We must not give room for domestic banterism where men are being butchered by their wives in their sleep-in order to ventilate their anger all in the name of fight for rights and privileges. Women, if we must fight, then we must tread with caution and protect the African race from extinction.

Peace
Yes!! We must tread with caution.

All
Yes!!! Dethrone Eshishi, dethrone Eshishi, dethrone Eshishi....
(*While they agitate, the narrator steps in*)

Narrator
O yes!!! Dethrone Eshishi (*Brief pause*). Dethrone Eshishi because irrespective of the fact that she earns herself and the women such tremendous victory, that is not how to win. Such shady antics of bribery, corruption, blackmail and all sorts of foul play can never be the best tool for any genus of revolution and development.
Yes, at the conclusion of Apogee, the women win, but if such victory is applauded then, we encourage the tool of social vices in facing our ordeals and if that be the case, in little or no time the decay of our society would have decayed beyond the state of Apogee.
(*At this juncture, the play fades out and is overtaken by dark and music*)

THE END

Broken Snail
Chika Onyashiyiwa Ose-Agbo

CHARACTERS
Sadiya: Rabiu's wife
Rabiu: Sadiya's husband
J. J.: Sadiya and Rabiu's son
Sanusi: Rabiu's brother
Doctor
Receptionist
Nurse
Eze: Ada's husband
Ada: Eze's wife
Papa: Eze's father
Udo: Eze's brother
Kinsmen- Young men of Uchegbu's family
Eno: a.k.a. Madam Destiny- Madame's customer
Levi: Madame's husband

Act I
Scene I

(Noon time. Rabiu is seated in front of his textile shop, he sees Sanusi passing by and calls out to him)

Rabiu:

Sanusi.

Sanusi:

Yes! How is business?

Rabiu:

What happened? You did not come back to the shop as we agreed earlier.

Sanusi:

I am sorry, when I got home my wife complained of severe headache so I decided to help her.

Rabiu:

Help her do what! House chores?

Sanusi:

When has it become a crime to help my own wife?

Rabiu:

My friend, very soon you will become your wife's errand boy.

Sanusi:

I rather become a happy errand's boy for my wife than otherwise.

Rabiu:

I cannot imagine myself doing a woman's work. What then is the need for a wife if she cannot serve me?

Sanusi:

On a more serious note, learn how to treat your wife right. This shouting, beating and lording will not give you a happy home. You are even lucky that Sadiya is calm and respects you a lot. Please stop taking her for granted.

Rabiu:
Haba Sanusi! If not that you are my brother, I would be suspecting you of coveting my wife. (Both men laugh heartily) Let me rush home and eat, I am very hungry. Later.

Sanusi:
See you at home then.

Scene II

(In a sparsely furnished sitting room with three long sofas, white and black transparent tiles adorning the floor and a Silver coloured 90" Hisense television sitting like a king on a brown tampered glass stand. A man enters, picks up the television remote and begins scanning the channels)

Rabiu:
J.J, where is your mother?
J.J:
She is in the kitchen.
Rabiu:
Diiiiiiii (Raising his voice slightly)
Sadiya:
Yes dear. Welcome. How was market today?
Rabiu:
Abeg, give me food.
Sadiya:
Give me few minutes, please.
(She goes back into the kitchen, few minutes later she comes out with a tray of food)
Rabiu:
(Washes his hands) Which soup?
Sadiya:
Abeg, eat food. Which soup will you not eat?
(Eating and watching television, Rabiu belches loudly) *(Sadiya hisses)* I have told you severally. This is a bad habit. You should know that your son is watching and learning.
Rabiu:

Shut that your dirty mouth! (*Sadiya murmurs*)
If I hear your voice, I will break this plate on your head.
Sadiya:
Try it again! I swear, you will regret it. *(As she bends down to carry the tray, her husband holds her throat tightly, choking her in the process. Their son starts crying as his mother struggles for breath. She eventually breaks free of his grip, without a word, she picks up the tray and goes back into the kitchen. A sobbing sound is heard from the kitchen meanwhile Rabiu is enjoying his favourite T.V programme. Mama J.J comes out from the kitchen with a big pestle, raises it high and hits her husband on his left shoulder. Panicked and in great pain, Rabiu struggles to stand up, Gbagam she hits him again on the back).*
Rabiu:
(In excruciating pain) Oh my God! Sadiya!! Have you gone crazy? Do you want to kill me? (*He tries to raise his left hand but could not.*)
Sadiya:
(*Raising the pestle towards his head*) Yes, I have gone mad. Let me kill you and go to jail.
Rabiu:
Sadiya! What are you doing? (*The pain on his shoulder and back worsening*)
Please put the pestle down. (*Shouting and groaning uncontrollably*) I'm dying oooo! J.J, go and call your uncle Sanusi.
Sadiya:
J. J! Go inside! (*Still brandishing her weapon*)
Rabiu:
Please help me, I am really dying.
Sadiya:

You think I am the only one meant to be dying. (*Staring menacingly*) Who cooks your food? Who washes your clothes? Who takes care of this house?

Rabiu:
Sadiya, I am sorry. Please help me.

Sadiya:
No! Stand up and beat me.

Rabiu:
I swear; I will never hit you again. Please! Please! (Curtain closes)

Scene III

(A building painted white and blue. Ladies in nurse's uniform going up and down the hallway. At the top of the building is the inscription in Neon "Chelsea Hospital". Rabiu is brought in on a wheel chair, screaming like a woman in labour.

Receptionist:
Hello ma, you are welcome. Can I have your card please?

Sadiya:
(Frisks through her bag in search of it.) It is not here, looks like I left it at home. *(Rabiu groans even louder)*

Receptionist:
Alright ma, that is not a problem. *(Hands her a sheet of paper)* Please write your file number or patient's full name here and wait to see the doctor. *(Sadiya writes the file number and goes to sit near Sanusi and Rabiu who is still groaning)*

Sanusi:
(Turning to Rabiu) Yaya, you see what I have been telling you. Look at what you have caused, just imagine the pain you are going through and how devastated Sadiya looks. It is your callousness and lack of respect and appreciation for your wife that have landed us in this hospital. What you are going through today is what you put your wife through most times, like a dog pushed to the wall, she has bitten you. You are my elder so I cannot reprimand you but I suggest you use your tongue to count your teeth.

Rabiu:

(*More to himself*) What have I done to myself? (*The receptionist rings a bell, points at them and they head to the doctor's office. Rabiu is wheeled in, as he cannot stand due to the pain in his back. An hour later, a nurse calls Rabiu's name, it was his turn to see the doctor.*)

Doctor:
Mr. Rabiu.

Rabiu:
Yes, Doctor

Doc:
What happened to you? Lie down let me examine you.
(*Looking at the masks on his back and shoulder he asked again*)
What happened, how did you get injured?

Rabiu:
It was a domestic accident, Doc.

Doctor:
I know it was an accident. I want to know the cause of the accident and how it happened.

Rabiu:
(*Visibly angered*) Doctor, I said it was an accident. It happened at home.

Sadiya:
(*Fidgeting*) Doc., Is it very serious?

Doctor:
Tell me what happened so I will know how to help you quickly.

Rabiu:
I fell down. I fell and hit my shoulder on the dining table.

Doctor:

You fell from a three storey building? My friend what happened to you? You did not fall. Mr. Rabiu, have you not heard that there are three persons that you must never lie to; your doctor, lawyer and priest? (*Rabiu keeps mute and stares at the ceiling.*)

Doctor:
Madam, I can sense your fear, what actually happened?

Sadiya:
(*Scared*) Doctor, I hit him with the pestle for pounding yam.

Doctor:
(*Wiping sweat from his brow*) This is serious! Your shoulder is dislocated.
(*Still feeling his vertebra*) Thank God, your back bone is not affected.

Sadiya:
(*Starts weeping*) See what you have caused, you made me almost lose my mind. Why do you like beating and humiliating me? I try my best to please you. If you no longer love me, divorce me before we kill each other

Rabiu:
Sadiya, am very sorry I didn't realize what you were going through.

Sadiya:
See the crazy thing you made me do, what if I had hit your head.

Rabiu:
Thank God, you didn't hit my head, please forgive me. I will be a better man for you.

Doctor:
(*Turning to Sadiya and Rabiu*) I want you both to learn from what happened today. Mr. Rabiu, you didn't stop to think of what would have happened if you had strangled your wife to death. If you are not aware, you would have been charged with murder and

sent to prison leaving your poor son in the mercy God knows who. Madam, the same fate would have befallen you if you had killed your husband. Anger and Violence are nobody's friend. Please learn how to talk to each other and talk things out. Dialogue is the best option in relationship matters. (*Sadiya continues weeping as the doctor prescribes some drugs and refers them to the orthopaedic section.*)

Scene IV
(The next day. Back at their home)
Rabiu:
(His shoulder in POP and sitting with back support, he calls out to his wife) Sadiya!
Sadiya:
Yes, dear. Do you need anything?
Rabiu:
No, just come and sit down here with me
Sadiya:
(Comes out from the room with a bottle of groundnut and sits beside him) My husband, we need to agree on what is acceptable and not acceptable in this relationship.
Rabiu:
You are right, Sadiya. I will have to work on my temper especially. I don't have any complaint about you. I need to unlearn some habits and learn new ones. For instance, instead of shouting and cursing you all the time, I will try talking to you gently the way you talk to me. I can learn to be useful or do I say be more present in my own home.
Sadiya:
(Surprised at Rabiu's words) Alhamdullah! My husband, may God keep me to see this new Rabiu.
Rabiu:
He will!
Rabiu:

You know what? That day the pain I felt made me have a rethink. As soon as my cast is removed, I will show you that I am a very good cook. I will neither divorce you nor hit you ever again. You saved me from turning into a real monster and a bad example for our son. I love you, my correct wife. You just take style to reset my brain.

Sadiya:
(*Sitting solemnly and lost in thoughts*) Baba J.J., that day, I almost died of fright. You didn't realize you were actually choking me to death. It was that fear that made me almost lose my mind. You know, I love you too, my husband. May The Almighty heal you speedily. (*Sadiya leaves the room*).

(Curtain falls)

Act 2

At a well-furnished tailor's shop. A tastefully dressed woman packs her 2019 model Toyota Highlander, alights and enters the shop. The owner of the shop, Madame, as she is fondly called, did not notice the arrival of one of her A-list customers as she is sitting on top of the sewing machine, engrossed in what she was sewing. She raised her head as she felt a touch on her shoulder. Looking up, she sees Eno smiling at her.

Madame:
Madam Destiny (*She owns a chain of Hotels called Destiny Suites.*) Abeg come inside.

Eno:
I just say make I greet you.

Madame:
Abeg come inside I wan tell you something.

Eno:
(*Enters and sits down.*) Ok.

Madame:
Will you be free this weekend? I wan make you come to our house, make you talk to my husband.

Eno:
OK, I know you don't want to talk here because of them. (*Pointing at the apprentices.*)

Madame:
Yes.

Eno:
Ok, I will come on Sunday.

Scene II

A sunny morning, in an open space in a face-me-I-face-you apartment. A woman is seen peddling her sewing machine under the neem tree. As Eno inches closer, the sound of her heels draws the attention of the women. Turning, she stands up from the machine as she sees Madam Destiny.

Madame:
Good morning, ma.

Eno:
Morning Madam, how are you today?

Madame:
Fine, ma. How is family?

Eno:
We are all fine. (*She brings a plastic chair for Eno to sit down on. An emaciated man walks past the two women hurriedly as if his life depended on avoiding them. Eno greets him. Without turning, he responds and increases his pace.*)

Eno:
Is that not your husband! What happened to him, where is he going to?
Is everything OK?

Madame:
(*feigning a smile.*) Madam Destiny, na one of the reasons wey make I wan see you. I hope say you get plenty time to listen to my story, so you fit advise me.

Eno:
Don't worry, today na Sunday so I no de go anywhere till evening.

Madame:
Thank you (*Smiling.*) Ma, you remember the other time wey you come my house?

Eno:
(*Trembling and shaking her head.*) How can I forget? With the condition I saw you in that day.
Madame:
Why are you shaking your head?
Eno:
Hmmmm! Each time I recall that day, I tremble with fear, I have always imagined myself in your shoe. Stressed emotionally and physically, stranded, robbed and the robbers threatening to throw my toddler into River Benue if I do not give them more money having taken my phones and handbag. Just picturing it in my mind given me the shivers. All for what? To please an insensitive and power drunk husband. God forbids! (*She circles her hand over her head and flicks her thumb and middle fingers together.*) My sister, let's stop poking old wounds.
Madame:
(*Laughing hysterically.*) Old wounds be that. Even though you no dey feel the pain, the wound wey don heal go dey look you *koro koro*. I called today make you hear wetin dey happen between Levi and me.
Eno:
(*Alarmed.*) Again! What did he do this time?
Madame:
Relax ma, no be pot only go dey cook goat, goat sef get power to dey break pot sef. Me sef don stand for my feet and dey answer my name join.
Eno:
(*Looking visibly relieved.*) Thank God.
Madame:

I no go ever forget that day, na the first time we I carry my marriage issue go meet third person. Me sef thank God say na you I carry the matter go meet. Your voice de hammer for my head every time I wan take decision. "Love your neighbour as yourself. Loving your husband, respecting your husband comes after you have love and respect for yourself, first".

Eno:
Did I really say that?

Madame:
You fit no remember but you talk am as water dey comot for your eyes dey flow for your face and you come hugged me join. That day na the day wey I know say I suppose stand on my leg. See me now, the result the show.

Eno:
(*Stands up with pride in her eyes, hugs Madame.*) I am proud of you.

Madame:
(*Surprised.*) Madam Destiny! (*Without saying anything Eno sits down.*) Na wetin be the matter, ma? I hope everything dey ok.

Eno:
No, don't worry (*Feigning a smiling.*) I am OK. What did you want to tell me?

Madame:
I go just start from the beginning. My husband begin gamble five years ago. In fact, na that be the beginning of his problem. Since wey I marry am, na me dey always bring food, na same me go cook am, I go pay children school fees and buy them clothes. He go only manage pay house rent while I go still pay NEPA bills and recharge DSTV. Rewind go July, 2020. Our landlord come

give us quit notice, make we commot, but my husband go meet am say him no go go anywhere.

Eno:
What are you saying?

Madame:
He even tell the man say he go fit beat am up and still carry am go court.

Eno:
What has gotten over Levi?

Madame:
E come reach April 2020, the landlord call me say make I choose whether I wan sacrifice one of my children to him abi I go leave his house. Landlord tell me say him dey tell me because I be beta person and he no get problem with me but if I follow my husband own, say I no go like wetin go happen to my children.

Na that day I make up my mind say I go leave Levi for there, pack my children and run. Na so I find this house pay for am and carry my five children alive leave Oga landlord house for am.

Eno:
What did Levi say?

Madame:
Levi! Levi dey flex muscle with landlord. Till the man use Civil Defense Officers with court notice pursue am. By Jan 2021 na so he pack him things come dey stay for here with us shamelessly.

Eno:
This is pathetic!

Madame:
E no pathetic oo, na freedom for me.

Now Levi na wife, me na husband. If food plenty and my children remain, they go give am chop. If nothing remain, he go sleep hungry. Now nothing wey Levi go fit boast of for this life except to watch Chelsea and do Bet Naija.

Eno:
Madame, how are you managing with all these wahala?

Madame:
Na God and determination. You know me now, I no dey go anywhere. Na my shop by 6 am to 7 pm every day.

Eno:
God will bless your children and all your labour. May God touch Levi!

Madame:
The reason wey make I come call you today, na to ask wetin I go do with Levi?
I wan carry m go court for divorce, but that my friend wey be banker say make I no divorce am, make I just allow am stay. Now, my problem na the wey he dey behave. Make him no come and die here one day.

(*As she is still speaking, Levi enters and stands with mouth open. Clearing her throat, Madame calls out to her husband mockingly.*)

My wife, you don come back? (*Eno turns to Levi.*)
Eno: Levi, are you back?

Levi:
(*Shamefully and without looking up.*) Yes, ma.
Eno: Please, come and sit down. (*Madame stands up to leave.*) No, don't leave, sit down please. Levi, how long have you been married?

Levi:

17 years.
Eno:
What is wrong with your wife?
Levi:
Nothing, ma.
Eno:
Feel free, Levi, am on your side.
Levi:
Nothing, ma, she has not done anything serious.
Eno:
Anything serious? That means she has been doing some things.
Levi:
(*Looking at Madame who was staring at the ground.*) It is not like that, what.
I meant is that whatever she has done is a reaction to what I did.
Eno:
Tell me about it.
Levi:
To be honest, my wife has always been good to me.
My problem with her started (*Staring at his wife.*) because I became envious of her and decided to suppress her to show her that I am a man.
Eno:
Is that so?
Levi:
Yes. Before now her ATM card used to be with me. She never disobeyed me. I used the money she makes however I wanted without her complaining. After I heard that she helped her brother buy Keke NAPEP I don't know what came over me.

Madame:
So that is the Problem?
How much be the keke? Six hundred and fifty thousand of which him don refund the three hundred thousand wey I been give am as loan.
How much I don dey give you since many years make you dey restock your shop? (*Raising her voice.*) Three hundred thousand every year since 1999. I no buy for you Toyota Corolla wey you no dey gree carried me inside.
Na who hear my voice the time when you collect my Ladies motorcycle wey me dey use after you sell your car?

Eno:
(*Surprised at this revelation.*)
Madame! Why did you not buy a plot of land with part of this money?
(*Realizing what she has just said she continued.*) We are not in a court.

Levi:
I know, but I am happy you are here.
If not, my wife never talks to me and it's killing me slowly.

Madame:
(*Hisses and murmurs to herself.*) Killing you slowly... Rubbish!

Levi:
Madam Destiny, help me beg my wife.

Madame:
(*Retorts angrily.*) Who be your wife?

Eno:
Relax Madame, let us resolve this matter.

Madame:
Before we go resolve anything, make him become man first,

because I dey see him like one riff-raff person.

Eno:
Don't say that.
(*Shamefaced, Levi puts his head down.*)

Levi:
Mummy, it is me oooo. Your Levi, your daddy.

Madame:
Now you don teach me lesson.
Make you hustle, get money, bring food, pay rent, pay children school fees and NEPA bills, the I go see the person wey dey talk.

Levi:
You know that my business has collapsed, I can't even pay the shop rent.

Madame:
Your shop collapse abi? Bet Naija don collapse your shop na.

Eno:
Levi, you have a lot of work to do. Disconnect yourself from betting.
I know you are addicted to it, but you can break free if you want.

Levi:
(*Heartbroken and downcast.*) I will try my best, ma.

Eno:
Don't try your best, work on yourself, I will help you talk to your wife.
Everything will be alright.

Levi:
Thank you, ma.

Madame:
Ma, but this is no be the reason wey make I called you come.

Eno:
Don't worry, everything will be alright. The same God that gave you this hot
yam will not allow it to scald your palm.
Madame: If you say so, thank you.
Eno:
Please, give me something to drink, I am thirsty.
(Madame goes out to get a drink for her. Curtain falls)

Act 3
Scene I

In a large compound with adjoining huts and a modern bungalow in the middle. An elderly man is seen sitting on a rocking chair in a dimly lit room opposite the bungalow. His eyes are slightly closed as he listens to his daughter-in-law.

Papa:
What did you say happened, Ada? I can't believe this; I never pushed his mother nor slapped her, not to talk of flogging her with belt.

Ada:
(*Wiping tears from her eyes.*) Some days, if I serve him food, he throws the soup at me and abuse me verbally. Since we got married, he has never given me money to buy anything for myself. Papa, you know the reason I am no longer working, it was because he wanted me to relocate so we can live together.

Papa:
Why did you have to tolerate him for the five years? No wonder you look older than your elder sister. (*Visibly angry*) No! This cannot continue. Don't worry, my daughter, go home, I must find a way to end this. (*Ada leaves the sitting room as Papa continues talking to himself.*)
(*Curtain falls.*)

Scene II

Two days later, at Uchegbu's compound. Papa Mike gathers the young men of the compound both married men and unmarried ones.

Papa:

(*Roaring in anger, papa stands.*) I have gathered you here to deal with a pressing issue. My son Eze has become a boxer who uses his wife as punching bag, he has become arrogant, foolish and self-conceited.

If anyone of you maltreats or is maltreating your wife, watch and learn (*He went inside his room and brought out a carton full of horsewhips, belts, twine, hand cuff, ground Cameroun pepper. He calls out to his daughter.*) Bring me one gallon of water and bowls. Eze and his wife are on the way.

All of you here will beat the demon off him.

Do not show him mercy before you are labelled kinsmen of a murderer.

(*As they were concluding the arrangements and strategy to deal with the erring husband, Eze and his wife drives in, gorgeously dressed in their tinted red Toyota Venza. As soon as he opened the door of his vehicle, he senses that something is amiss.*)

Eze:

(*Walking straight to his father who is looking sorrowful.*) Papa what is it?

Papa:

Eze, it is you. I mean you who have become a wife beater.

Eze:

(*Confused, he looked at his brother, Udo. His father spits on his face and stands up.*)

Papa:

Udo.

Udo:
Papa.
Papa:
This is your brother, cure him of his madness. (*As soon as papa turns his back, they all descend on him. It is a collective beating - Utu aka – as his people call it. Slaps from all angles, whips, peppered water poured on his head. His eyes biting. In a split second the almighty Eze is on the ground screaming.*)
Eze:
My eyes oo. What have I done oo! Papa! Papa ooo! My eyes, I can't see oo! Please! Please!
(*His shirt is torn off his body, different shapes of whips marks on his body, his face and his body swollen. After 35 minutes of the family beating, Eze lost consciousness. Meanwhile, his wife is crying and shouting for help, but nobody dares interfere, it is papa's decision.*)
Ada:
Papa Eze is dead!
Papa:
(*Showing no sign of panic*) It is okay, feel his chest.
Udo:
He is breathing.
Papa:
Coward! Take him to the hospital. If anybody asks, tell them his father disciplined him.
(*Few days later, Eze is back to his father's house alive. As he enters the sitting room his father who is reading a newspaper dropped it and stands up to leave the room.*)
Papa:
(*Sneering at Eze.*) Onye uchu! (Shameless man)

Eze:
(*Humbly walking towards his father, broken.*) Papa, Papa. forgive me. (*Kneeling down he held onto his father hands.*) Biko (Please) Papa. I lost my myself. I don't have any excuse for treating my wife badly. You know how much I love her. I was just afraid of losing her.

Papa:
(*Refusing to look at him.*) Leave this old man's hand before you pull it off the socket.

Eze:
(*As if his father's word pierced his heart, he quickly left his hand and put his face on his feet, devastated.*) Paaapaa. I know I have disappointed you gravely, knowing how much you love, and support my mum. Papa, Please. Never again, I swear on my life.

Papa:
A real man does not beat a woman, he loves and supports his woman. Your wife is a reflection of yourself. Why should you turn my beautiful and self-confident Ada to an old and beggarly woman?

Eze:
Am sorry, papa. I will compensate her for the pain.

Papa:
In a marriage, there is bound to be misunderstanding because both of you are two strangers trying to understand each other. The solution is neither abuse nor violence. Sit your wife down and talk things out. You are lucky, Ada is a great woman. In spite of what you put her through, she never stopped smiling nor respecting you.

Eze:

(*Profusely weeping.*) Papa, my fears blinded me to all her good qualities.

Papa:
Eze, my son.

Eze:
Papa

Papa:
Find a job for Ada. Treat her as if you were still courting her and all your fears will go away.

Eze:
(*Sobbing.*) Papa. (*Brings out an envelope from his breast pocket.*). This is Ada's appointment letter. I knew you will ask me to do it, so I decided to do it to show you that your son is back.

Papa:
Eze, when you beat your wife, you are also beating yourself. Treat your wife the way you would like to be treated and she will never go against you in this life or the one after.

Eze:
Thank you, Papa. (*Stands up.*) Am coming. (*Calling out to his sister.*) Adaugo, come. (*He brings out the food stuffs he bought for his parents: a bottle of Verga Silica, a beautiful walking stick, a red cap and a matching white jumper top and presents them to his father.*) Papa, I have brought them to thank you for reminding me whose son I am.

Papa:
(*Smiling with pride, places his hand on his head to bless him.*) Son, I know the apple cannot fall far from the tree. May it be well with you. Take good of your wife, we make mouth with our wives never forget that. May you and your wife prosper. Go and enjoy your home.

Eze:
(*Beaming with smiles.*) Thank you, Papa.
Papa:

Adaugo, bring something for my son to drink.
(*Curtain falls.*)

Scene III

Few weeks later, At the wedding reception of Madam Destiny's daughter. The doctor notices Sadiya and walks towards their table, she is sharing the table with her husband and another couple- Madame and Levi. The doctor draws a seat and sits down.

Doctor:

How are you, Madam? You look gorgeous (turning to her husband) I hope you don't mind.

Rabiu:

Not at all, Sir. In fact, I am very happy to see you. I have not had the opportunity to thank for the advice you gave us. (*Smiling warmly*) It has really helped us and still helping us.

Doctor:

I am pleased to hear this. A happy and peaceful marriage do not just happen, it comes through hard work, patience, tolerance, understanding and empathy (*Levi looks at his wife and whispered something to her and both of them laugh*)

Levi:

You are very correct, sir. It is hard work indeed!
(*Laughing heartily, all stand and raise their glasses for a toast. The voice of Madam Destiny is heard ringing "to a happy and prosperous home"*)
(*All chorus cheers!*)

Light fades.

The end.

The Mirage, or *The Vast Misenlightenment of Andy Ntia*
Itunuoluwa Williams

Plot

Aniekan "Andy" Ntia – a homegrown Efik man – returns home to Calabar where his arrival has been highly anticipated for years. Before leaving for the US, Andy was already engaged to his childhood sweetheart Idara. Since his departure 5 years ago, Idara has passed through the *nkuho* – an Efik tradition – and has emerged fat, the local standard of beauty. To the Efik, she is beautiful, radiant, and would be the pride of any warm-blooded man. However, Andy does not concur as he elects to marry Angela, a slim white American woman who does not always respect and embrace his culture. What ensues is a comedy of sorts, as we explore Andy's newly found aversion to fat. This project is borne out of Fat Studies, a branch of Body Theory that focuses on research and practice of fat bodies, and how being fat intersect with other aspects of one's individual identity such as race, gender, sexuality, and socioeconomic status.

Disclaimer

While this play is written in English, I have included a number of Efik and popular Nigerian phrases and expressions to infuse some cultural authenticity and realism into this work. To that extent, I have included a glossary with comprehensive definitions of the non-English words and phrases used for the audience's convenience. Additionally, I have written this from the perspective of Nigerian English, which is typically a mix of indigenous languages and pidgin English (a form of creole spoken in West Africa) with the English language. All the phrases included should be easily understandable with the help of the glossary and taking into account the context.

CAST

Idara: The heroine. A dark skin, average-height accountant who has recently emerged from the fattening room. Idara is looking forward to the next stage of her life, having awaited Andy's return from America. Originally 160 lbs, her time in the *nkuho* (fattening room) has caused her to gain 40 lbs more, making her more curvaceous and beautiful by Efik standards.
Andy: aka Aniekan Ntia. The male protagonist, Andy, has recently returned from America. Before leaving for America, he was involved with Idara, a young woman from his community.
Angela: Andy's "friend". She is a white, tall, slender 20-something-year-old. While she is not evil in the slightest, she can be oblivious to Efik cultural norms or social cues in general and often discourages Andy from speaking his mother tongue around her.
Mama Ani: Andy and Idongesit's mother, an often dramatic but likable woman.
Idongesit: Andy and Etim's sister, Mama Ani's only daughter.
Godspower: Andy's childhood friend; fondly called "Godii".

Uncle Okon: Family friend, no one is sure how he's related to the family.
Itoro: Idara's younger sister.
Mama Idara: Idara and Itoro's mother.
Etim: Andy and Idongesit's younger brother, Mama Ani's youngest child.
Narrator

GLOSSARY
Abasi: God; Abasi ikana: God forbid
Abeg: Popular Nigerian slang for "Please"
Abi: Popular Nigerian slang, similar to the use of "yeah", "right", "or" in English
Adiaha: First daughter; adiaha mmi: My first daughter
Afia mma mmi: My white woman
Amebo: Slang used to refer to a busybody who loves gossip, or the act thereof
Bum-bum: Pidgin for buttocks
Chop: Slang for food or to eat
Ebod: Goat
Emedi: Welcome
Harmattan: Refers to the strong, dry dusty wind that blows from the Sahara desert to West Africa between November to February. Harmattan season is marked by cold windy mornings and nights and very hot middays, depending on the locale.
Idara-abasi: Meaning "the joy of God"
Idara mmi: My joy
Idem fo: How are you?
Ikut enyin: Long time no see

Ima mmi: My love
Ìnín: Sorry
Lepa: A popular Nigerian slang meaning "slim", "slender" or "thin"
Masquerade: A popular series that aired on Nigerian television till the mid-1990s. Apena was a recurring character.
Mbakara mmi: "My Oyibo". In Nigeria, Oyibo is a popular slang used to refer to a white person.
Mbopo mmi: My pride; fresh wife material
Mesiere: "Hello", the general form of greeting in Efik
Mimm Ukop Iko: This is a letter sent with bottles of drinks by a man's family to a lady's family to declare his intentions for marriage. The lady's family makes a decision before sending a reply with permission for them (the man and his family) to visit at a chosen date.
Mkpouto mmi: My pride or Precious
Mme ama fi: I love you
Naija: Slang referring to the country Nigeria
Naira: Nigerian currency
Nau: Slang used to emphasize a point
Ndoko mma: Beauty Queen
NEPA: Acronym for the National Electric Power Authority, refer to the previous but still popular term used to refer to Nigeria's electricity governing organization. NEPA pole refers to wooden power poles used for generating and transmitting electricity; they are usually very tall and slim in build.
Nkuho: Means "seclusion" or "confinement", refers to the "fattening room/house". According to Efik custom, a lady is secluded in the ufok nkuho for a period before marriage; there she is fattened up - fat being the traditional standard of beauty among

Efiks - and prepared for marriage, childbirth and rearing, and participating in the adult age group in her community. Traditionally, an Efik woman must "enter into *nkuho*" at least once in her lifetime.

Nsi tipe: What happened here?

Obonghwan mi: My Queen

Ọfọn o: Reply to "thank you"

Oya: A popular Nigerian slang meaning "okay" or "let's go"

Sha: A popular conversation slang in Nigeria, it does not really have a meaning.

Sọsọngọ: Thank you

Tre: Stop

Udiong Ufok: The introduction ceremony, this event occurs after the Mimm Ukop Iko has been received and the lady's family has given permission to the man's family to visit. This formalizes the man's intentions to marry the lady and all her family members are present to witness the occasion. Afterwards, he is given a list of marriage gifts and requirements according to Efk tradition.

Ugu: Pumpkin leaves, a popular leafy green used in Nigerian cuisine

Utuenikang mmi: My light

Uyai mbopo: Translates to the "beauty of the fattened girl"

Yansh: Nigerian slang for buttocks or the hip area in general

Prelude: MME AMA FI

Stage lights up. Two voices are heard arguing behind the curtains.

Voice 1:
Wait, wait *nau*. Let's talk.

Voice 2:
Mister man, I've told you that we don't have anything to talk about, stop following me.

Voice 1:
But why won't I follow you dear? I have to at least try. *Idara mmi*, please listen to me.

Voice 2:
[*loud whisper*] *Tre*, stop it! Don't mention my name, what if someone hears you? And keep your voice down please.

Voice 1:
[*somewhat subdued*] I'm sorry *nau*, I didn't mean to make you angry. But you know it's not easy for me, I've been trying to tell you how I feel for a while now.

Voice 2:
[*sighs exasperatedly*] Okay, I'm listening.

Voice 1:
[*Begin praising* Voice 2] *Ima mmi, utuenikang mi, obonghwan mmi*. My dear, let me people send *Mimm Ukop Iko* to your kinsmen *nau*.

Voice 2:
[*Startled*] Ehn? What are you saying, stop it please!

Voice 1:
My dear, have you ever known me to be a liar? A cheater? Someone who cannot be trusted? Even you, you know that I am a responsible man and I'm willing and able to take care of you, let our kinsmen meet and talk.

Voice 2:
No, that cannot happen. Come, why are you talking like this? You know I'm a taken woman, my intended and I have already done the *Udiong Ufok*, our kinsmen have agreed, I just came out of the *nkuho*, all that's left now is the *ndo*.

Voice 1:
[*bitterly*] Yes yes, I know. But that was some 5 years ago, what is taking him forever?

Voice 2:
[*definitively*] Please stop it. That is none of your business.

Voice 1:
Okay okay… anyway, I am not concerned about him, I only care about you and me, what we have and what we can become.

Voice 2:
Ohhhhh *Abasi*, help me. What we have??? *Broda*, we don't have anything o, I'm an engaged woman, I take God beg you.

Voice 1:
Come on, you can't deny that there's something between us. I feel it and my dear, I know you feel it too or else, that incident would have never hap….

Voice 2:
[*abruptly cuts him off, pleadingly*] Imoh, I use God beg you, please forget that day, it was a moment of weakness. I have struggled with the guilt since that day, please don't bring it up at all. In fact, it never happened, [*emphatically*] nothing happened, absolutely nothing.

Voice 1:
[*downcast*] That's not fair to me but okay. But at least let my kinsmen call on your Papa.

Voice 2:
[*slightly raised*] And tell my Papa what? Tell him what? That their son wants to marry his daughter? The same daughter that he has already done introduction for? The daughter that he's waiting to finalize her marriage arrangements? What do you think he'll say? How would he react, my Papa that has high blood pressure. What would I tell my husband's family, that I'm not doing again, that they should come and collect their gifts *abi*? What will people think? I would be seen as a wayward woman in this town, and you'll be labeled a wife snatcher. Is that what you want?

Voice 1:
I know it's complicated and might be very difficult but if I'm with you and you're with me, I think it's worth it.

Voice 2:
Ahn ahn no! Mister Romeo, NO. I am not your Juliet. Please, go and find another person to marry, there are plenty of good ladies in this community. I will continue waiting for my husband, it won't be long now.

A brief silence ensues.

Voice 1:
[*sighs in defeat and says wearingly*] Alright my dear, I give up, clearly you don't want me. But I must say…

Voice 2:
What?

Voice 1:
Your intended is a big fool. In fact, he must be in a trance to have kept you waiting this long. But how I envy him because he will have you to wake up to.

SCENE 1: MESIERE
Lights on, curtain open. Enter Andy
Narrator:
Aniekan "Andy" Ntia arrives at Airport, Calabar, Cross River state, Nigeria after a 23-hour flight from LaGuardia Airport, NY. At 30 years old, he stands at 5'10 and weighs 185 lbs. From his slight muffin top, it is obvious that he needs to cut back on his alcohol intake and eating. While he looks like an average joe, he has lovely caramel skin and a bright smile whenever he chooses to unleash it in full force. The year is 1997 and Andy has been in America for the past 5 years where he received his master's degree and began working as a civil engineer in New York City. His family has missed him terribly and Uncle Okon and Andy's childhood friend Godspower (Godii) have come to collect him up from the airport. Andy is currently standing in the airport lobby with a luggage cart holding several bags. However, he has not returned alone…

Enter Angela

Angela:
Andy, be careful with those bags, please! We don't want to ruin your mum's presents. [*sighs exasperatedly*] Oh my God, what a flight! I'm so tired and ready for a good soak.

Andy:
A whole international airport and no electricity. [*he shakes his head ruefully*] Nigeria, we hail thee indeed!

Angela:
Is our ride here yet? My skin feels like ants are crawling all over. Can you call them to rush down to pick us up?

Andy:

Angela baby, I've told you before that international calls don't work like that, they're really expensive. Anyway, they should be here by now; I telegraphed Godi our flight itinerary months ago.

Angela:
Why is everyone staring at me? Do I have something on my face? Did I drool in my sleep?

Andy:
[*laughs*] No, Angela. It's because many of them have never seen a white woman before, hmm. *Mbakara mmi, Afia mma mmi* [*he says lovingly*].

Angela:
[*blushes*] Why do you always sound funny when you speak that language? I've told you countless times to address me only in English, it makes you sound smarter.

Andy smiles to himself as he swivels his head, looking for his friend.

Aside:
Uncle Okon *and* Godspower *are also in the lobby, scanning the crowd for* Andy. Godspower *is holding a cardboard sign with his friend's name on it.*

Uncle Okon:
Godii, you don see am? All dis plenty people dey turn my eye.

Godspower:
Uncle I'm looking, they should be here by now. They already announced that the flight has landed. Let me raise the sign again, maybe they can't see it.

Uncle Okon:
Oya, raise am, raise am.

Godspower *raises the sign above his head, his long arms working to his advantage.* Angela *sees the sign and calls* Andy's *attention.*

Angela:
Andy, isn't that your name? That must be your friend.
Andy:
Oh yes, that's me [*raises his voice and hand to get* Godspower's *attention*] Godii Godii!
Godspower *notices* Andy *and calls* Uncle Okon's *attention.*
Godspower:
Uncle, I see him, see him there by the stand. [*shouts happily*] Ani Ani!!!
Uncle Okon:
Ehh he's here. [*clasps hands together and looks up in thanks*] *Abasi sọsọngọ.*
Andy *races to meet* Uncle Okon *and* Godspower, *all three are clearly very excited*
Godspower:
Ani the Anthill!
Andy:
Godspower the NEPA pole! Baba Goody Goody!!
They laugh and shake hands, slapping each other on the back emphatically.
Godspower:
Emedi my friend, you've been missed.
Andy:
Godii Godii, it's good to see you dis guy.
Godspower:
How have you been *nau*?
Andy:
Good, we thank God. How is family? Bad guy, how far that your babe Eno?
Godspower:

[*blushes*] She dey, she dey. Everybody is fine, we thank God.
Andy *notices* Uncle Okon *and goes to greet him.*

Andy:
Ahh [*bends head in greeting*] *mesiere* Uncle Okon.

Uncle Okon:
[*Nods in approval while tapping* Andy's *shoulder*] Aniekan my boy! *Ikut enyin*, you don't want to see us again *abi?* You've been enjoying America too much. You've forgotten all about us, ehn? [*laughs*] *Idem fo?*

Andy:
[*he smiles brittlely. He is clearly uncomfortable with* Uncle Okon's *accusations but hides it well*] *Idem mi ọsọñ*, good to see you Uncle.
Uncle Okon *notices* Angela *lurking in the background.*

Uncle Okon:
Ahn ahn, who own dis *oyibo?* *Oyibo,* you don lost?
Andy, who *realizes* Uncle Okon *must be referring to* Angela*, suddenly remembers her and rushes to make the introductions.*

Andy:
No Uncle, she's with me. Angela, this is Uncle Okon and my very good friend Godspower, Godii, the one I've been telling you about. Uncle Okon, Godii, this is Angela, my fi…friend [*smiles apologetically at* Angela *who regards him strangely*].
Angela *puts out her hand to shake* Uncle Okon*, a brazen move deemed disrespectful to elders in Nigeria.*

Uncle Okon:
[*laughs uncomfortably but takes her hand*] Ehen? How are you, my dear? You're welcome.

Angela:
It's good to meet you Uncle Okon, thank you!

[Angela *moves to* Godspower *who is expecting to shake hands too. He is shocked when* Angela *pecks his cheeks instead, freezing him on the spot.* Uncle Okon *looks pleasantly confused as if watching a comedy unfold.* Meanwhile, Andy *grimaces like a teacher disappointed in his favorite student*].

Angela:
And Godii, it's great to meet you! I've heard so much about you that I feel like I know you already!

Godspower:
[*chuckles uncomfortably*] Hehe…you're welcome.

Uncle Okon:
Indeed your name is Angela, you look like an angel among men [*laughs at his joke as* Angela *demures*]. Maybe if you have a younger sister or cousin in your family, you can introduce me so that I too can have an angel for …
Sensing the uncomfortable atmosphere, Godspower *interrupts.*

Godspower:
Okay Uncle Okon. Ani, are you ready to go?

Andy:
[*visibly relieved*] Oh yes, please let's go before there's traffic on the road.

Godspower:
Have you forgotten where you are? [*chuckles*] This is Naija, there's always traffic.

Andy:
[*sucks his teeth*] Mtchew, it's true sef.
Godspower *leads the way and exits while* Andy *and* Angela *follow, whispering between themselves.*

Angela:

Really? Friend? Why didn't you just call me buddy and fistbump me too?

Andy:

Shh... Okay sorry but I told you we have to tell them gently, now is not the time. And why did you greet them like that? I told you that's not the proper way to greet people here, especially elders. *Mesiere...*[enunciates] *ME-SEI-RE*, I've told you.

Angela:

[*protests*] Oh I've told you that saying those words make me feel silly. Besides, they seemed to understand me well enough. If it's good in America, it should be good here too.

Andy:

[*slightly miffed*] That's enough, let's go.

Andy *puts his hand around her shoulder as they exit the stage.* Uncle Okon *who is behind them and notices the gesture laughs to himself.*

Uncle Okon [*laughs*] *Abasi* o, dis boy has gone to get himself an *oyibo*. Ahhh, Mama Ani go kill person o, na me talk am first! Anyway *sha*, let me see if *oyibo* has an Angelica or Angelina back in America so that I can have my own *afia mma mmi* too. Okon Okon, you're on point, very good!

Shakes his head gleefully and begins whistling a tune as he exits. Lights dim, curtain falls.

SCENE 2: EDIKANG IKONG

Lights brighten, curtains lift to reveal Mama Ani *and* Idongesit.

Narrator:

Mama Ani is the matriarch of the Ntia family. An expressive and vocal woman currently in her 50s, she is well-built in stature, a figure she credits to her time in the *nkuho* (fattening room) as a young lady. She has eagerly awaited her son's arrival back home and is excited for his return for more reasons than one. She is currently putting her chopped *ugu* leaves into a large pot where she has been making *edikang ikong*, a staple Efik vegetable soup rich in protein. With her is her daughter Idongesit, laboring but efficiently pounding the yam for the dish.

Idongesit:

[*singing*] *Abasi nmi ayaya o, ayaya o;* [*pounds*] *Abasi nmi ayaya o ayaya anana ndo* x2

Mama Ani:

Tre Idongesit! How many times have I told you not to sing or talk when pounding yam? It's like you want everybody to eat your saliva tonight *abi?*

Idongesit:

[*slightly breathlessly*] Ah no! *Inín* Mama. [*pounds*] I'm just so excited because Bro Ani is finally coming home.

Mama Ani:

[*smiles*] Ehh yes, you're right my dear. I don't know why he hasn't come home since. I thought I would have to go and bring him back from America myself. I even had to send your late father in my dream to tell his son to come home [Idongesit *secretly rolls her eyes at this comment*] What is keeping him there? It's not like those people know how to make *edikang ikong* with their hand butter and plenty-plenty sweets.

Idongesit:

[*thoroughly amused, momentarily stops pounding*] Mama! It is HAM-BURGER oh, not HAND-BUTTER. There's nothing like that.

Mama Ani:

Ehn HAND-BUTTER *abi* HAND-BURGER, whatever they call it. With all their candy and sweets that are bad for the teeth and the body. A real man needs real food. [*smiles with motherly pride*] And my Aniekan is a real man.

Idongesit *smiles and shakes her head as she resumes pounding. By now, she's used to her mother's theatrics.*

Mama Ani:

[*stirs the soup and tastes it, nodding her head in approval*] Yes, the *edikang ikong* is ready now. I know this is his favorite. By the time Aniekan tastes this, let's see if he'll run away to America again [*she turns off the stove and grins at the pot like a witch staring at her cauldron, pleased with her mind-altering concoction*].

Idongesit:

Yes Mama, you're right. [*pounds*] And finally, we can alert Papa Idara…

Mama Ani:

My dear, it's as if you're in my mind. We've kept the Inyangs waiting long enough. I cannot keep coming up with stories to put them off, I don't want them thinking we're dishonorable people, *Abasi ikana*!

Idongesit:

[*slightly breathless*] And *sista* Idara too… [*stops pounding to inspect the pounded yam*]

Mama Ani:

[*Proudly*] *Mbopo mmi*! The first among women! Idara-abasi, she is truly the embodiment of her name! [*she praises* Idara *while* Idongesit *nods and smiles in agreement*] Yes, she would truly be the chief jewel in Aniekan's crown. That reminds me…[*shouts*] Etim!

A teenage boy, Etim, *enters.*

Mama Ani:
Go down and tell the Inyangs that we'll be coming to greet them with wine very soon. We should be there Saturday morning by 10.
Etim:
[*giddily*] Heh, yes Mama [*runs off*].
Mama Ani:
[*calls after him*] Come straight home o! I don't want to be looking up and down for you this evening.
Etim *leaves to deliver the message at the* Inyang *house.*
Idongesit:
Finally the matter will be settled. And remember her coming out ceremony last month?
Mama Ani:
Ahhhhh! *Uyai mbopo!* She was so beautiful my chest was swelling with pride. The fairest of them all, like Smoke White.
Idongesit:
[*Utterly confused*] Smoke White??? What is that?
Mama Ani:
You know, Smoke White, the princess with the evil stepmother in the stories [Idongesit *bursts out laughter*] What, why are you laughing?
Idongesit:
[*still laughing*] Mama, you'll not kill me. It's SNOW-WHITE, not Smoke White [*continues laughing*].
Mama Ani:
[*slightly miffed*] Whatever. You're still talking over the pounded yam! if I should see your saliva in my food *ehn*!
Idongesit:
Calm down Mama, it's ready.

Mama Ani:
[*feels the pounded yam's texture and agrees grudgingly, she was hoping to scold* Idongesit *some more*] Alright, well done. Don't worry, you'll find a good man soon too but for now, face your book o! [Idongesit *blushes*] Oya go get dressed and make sure everything is arranged while I finish up here.

Idongesit:
Alright Mama [*exits*].

Mama Ani:
[*singing*] *Abasi nmi ayaya o, ayaya o; Abasi nmi ayaya o ayaya anana ndo*

Aside:
Andy *and the rest have arrived at the house and knock on the door.* Idongesit *opens the door and is delighted to see her older brother; the two embrace. Having heard the noise,* Mama Ani *comes out to investigate only to discover her son.*

Andy:
[*equally delighted*] Mama [*moves to hug his mother*].

Mama Ani:
[*choked up with happy tears*] Aniekan! *Emedi* my son!

Andy:
Mama, I've missed you.

Mama Ani:
[*playfully pushes him away*] Shut up this boy. If you missed me so much, why are you just coming back home? What if I had died and joined your late father and elder brother with *Abasi*? Idongesit would have had to bury me all by herself like I'm an outcast [Idongesit *rolls her eyes exasperated with her mother while* Andy *looks on fondly*]. Everyone would laugh at me, the woman whose son abandoned her after going to America.

Andy:
[*chuckles and hugs his mother fondly*] Oh Mama, never change. I did miss you.
Mama Ani:
[*somewhat mollified but fakes annoyance*] Oh please. As if I don't know that you've only come back for Idara. Don't worry, the matter has been arranged, we'll be calling on them on Saturday morning.
Andy:
[*laughs uneasily*] Not now Mama. Another time.
Mama Ani *looks momentarily confused but* Andy *continues.*
Andy:
[*moves to* Angela] Mama, I would like to introduce you to Angela, my very dear friend [Uncle Okon *and* Godspower *exchange odd looks while* Idongesit *looks sharply as if analyzing a difficult math problem*]. Angela, this is my mother *Mama* [*looks at* Angela *as if his next words are specifically for her*]… greet her PROPERLY.
Angela:
[*initially looks miffed but recovers quickly*] [*uneasily*] Mezzy-ere Mama.
Mama Ani:
[*scrutinizes* Angela *from head to toe but replies warmly*] *Mesiere* my dear, you're welcome. *Idem fo?*
Angela:
[*blushes in embarrassment*] Oh sorry, I don't understand…
Andy:
Mama, Angela doesn't speak Efik, please address her in English.
Angela:
Yeah sorry, [*enunciates her words like* Mama Ani *is a fool*] no speak Efik, too many mumbling words, I'll look stupid [*laughs while the room grows quiet at her unintentional slight*].

Mama Ani:
[*Unimpressed*] Hmm. You're welcome my dear. Don't worry, we all speak English well. Do you work with Aniekan in engineering too? [*slightly excited*] That's very good, women belong in these types of professions just as much as men, I'm always telling Idongesit.
Angela:
Oh no, I couldn't with all those graphs and lines and math. My head might explode.
Mama Ani:
Okay. What do you do then, tell me?
Angela:
I'm actually in between jobs right now. But in my free time, I moonlight as a hairdresser and I model sometimes.
Mama Ani *scrutinizes* Angela *again like the guardian angel of heaven deliberating if she was worthy to pass through the pearly gates. In the background,* Idongesit *shoots a questioning look at* Godspower *who shrugs helplessly.*
Mama Ani:
[*recovers*] Okay. [*turns attention to* Godspower *who's almost caught off-guard*] Godii! Sọsọngọ my son. Idem fo?
Godspower:
[*respectfully*] Ọfọn o Mama Ani, we're all happy to…
Uncle Okon:
[*interrupts* Godspower] Mama Ani if you're still planning to die, please give us *chop* before you go so that we don't follow you immediately. Some of us are not ready.
Mama Ani:
Okon, one of these days, I'll poison you myself, you hear?
Uncle Okon:

Woman, add all the poison you want, my stomach would neutralize it [*laughs and pats his stomach fondly*].

Mama Ani:

[*clicks teeth*] Mtchew, nonsense. [*turns to* Andy, *smiles*] I made your favorite - pounded yam and *edikang ikong*. I'm sure you've missed it after all these years. You look so skinny, aren't they feeding you in America?

Andy:

[*laughs*] Mama I'm not skinny oh, see my stomach. And AHHHHH, *edikang ikong*, I'M READY Mama!

Mama Ani:

Hahaha! Trust me *nau*, I'm coming. Idongesit! [*gestures to the kitchen*] [*turns to* Andy and Angela] You two can quickly freshen up while we set the table. Godii please help them. Okon, don't eat that old fruit, you're not a goat! [Uncle Okon *drops a dull-colored apple like a deer caught in headlights*].

Mama Ani *and* Idongesit *exit.*

Godspower:

Let me go get the other bags out of the car [*exits*].

Angela:

What're we eating?

Andy:

Edikang ikong and pounded yam. Don't worry, you'll love it [*chef's kiss*].

Angela:

[*unsure*] Okay let's see. I hope it doesn't ruin my figure. You know I don't want to be fat, that's just ugly.

The two disappear - the lights dim.
Lights come back on.

Everyone is seated save for Mama Ani, Idongesit, *and* Godspower. Andy *and* Angela *have changed into more casual clothes.* Andy *and* Uncle Okon *are visibly excited as they await their meal. Enter* Idongesit *and* Mama Ani *with dishes of pounded yam and edikang ikong,* Godspower *follows behind with a bowl of water for handwashing and hand towels.*

Uncle Okon:
Aha! Time to eat. Godii, pass the water and towel, please.

Just as everyone is dishing their portions, Angela *exclaims as* Idongesit *serves her.*

Angela:
No no no! I won't be eating that, no thank you.

Mama Ani:
Ehn, what's the problem, are you okay?

Andy:
Babe, what's the problem? [Idongesit *and* Godspower *exchange shocked looks,* Andy *has clearly made a sleep of tongue*].

Angela:
I can't eat that. That thing [*points at the pounded yam*] looks like a big hard ball of mashed potatoes that would sit in my tummy and make me fat. And that [*points to the soup*], why does it smell so bad? [*wrinkles nose*]

Idongesit:
Oh no, it doesn't smell bad, that's just the aroma of the food, the seasoning that you're smelling. That means it tastes good.

Angela:
Well I don't care what it is, take it away, please. Can I get something else to eat?

Idongesit:

[*looks slightly offended*] But Mama and I spent all day preparing this. I pounded the yam myself while Mama made the soup, you really should try it, even if it's just the soup alone.

Angela:
I'm sure you ladies put a lot of time into making this but I won't be having any of it, it would ruin my figure.

Idongesit:
[*whispers under her breath*] What figure? You have none, no yansh, no breast.

Andy:
[*cautions his sister*] Idongesit. [*turns to* Angela] You're sure you don't want to try this? Even if it's just the soup?

Angela:
No I can't. And you really shouldn't either, you'll get fat.

Andy:
[*sighs and turns to his mother*] Mama, can we get something else to eat please?

Godspower:
We?! Ani, you won't be eating either?

Andy:
No, Angela is right. I really shouldn't [*looks longingly at the dish, after all, it's his favorite*].

Idongesit:
But we made this specially for YOU. See, there are even snails inside, very big ones.

Andy:
[*visibly pained, he manages to say*] No Idongesit, I'm sure [*turns to* Mama Ani] Can we get something else, please? Maybe some rice and stew?

Angela:
No, no rice please, that'll make me look puffy in the morning and give me a big bum the size of Texas. Can we get a salad instead? Just some spinach and tomatoes. And no dressing please, that's bad for you.

Idongesit:
So...like an *ebod*?

Mama Ani:
[*in a calm and level voice*] Idongesit, that's enough. Please take the rest away and go see if we have any *ugu* or spinach and fresh tomatoes left and chop them up. I'll join you shortly.

Idongesit:
[*looks like she wants to protest but chooses to respect her mother's instructions*] Alright Mama [*mumbles under her breath in Efik*].

Godspower:
[*gets up*] I'll help her.

Mama Ani: [*in a calm but commanding voice*] No Godii, sit and eat your food, sọsọñọ my son [*she says while looking at* Andy *who doesn't meet her gaze*]. I'll go.

Angela:
Awesome, thank you, Mama. So sorry again.

Mama Ani:
Hmm. [*exits*]

Uncle Okon:
[*yells for* Idongesit] Idongesit, bring the remaining *edikang ikong* and pounded yam. If they don't want it, I'm here, we can't all be starving please.

Mama Ani *heads for the kitchen but stops short in the corridor leading to it, where she stares at* Idongesit *who's working in complete silence, her lips set in a hard line, her movements jerky*

Mama Ani:
[*under her breath*] Papa Aniekan, what's happening?

In the background,

Uncle Okon:
[*shouts*] Idongesit!

Lights dim, curtain falls.

SCENE 3: UYAI MBOPO

Curtain lift to reveal the Inyang *family house. The audience is introduced to* Idara.

Narrator:

Idara Inyang is sitting in her room, doing some calculations. A Certified Public Accountant working at a consultancy firm in Calabar, she recently returned home to pass through the *nkuho* (fattening room). At 27yrs old, she is the *adíaha* (first daughter) of the family and is beloved by her family and the townspeople for her professional accomplishment, grace, and beauty. Along the walls are records of ABBA, Blondie, Queen, Elton John, the Beatles; clearly she's a fan. She is currently working on the daily budget ahead of the Christmas festivities. Next to her is a bowl of boiled peanuts to snack on, a habit she recently developed from her time in the fattening room.

Idara:

[*singing*] "The tide is high but I'm holdin' on; I'm gonna be your number one; I'm not the kinda girl who gives up just like that, oh no"

Enter Itoro, Idara's *younger sister*

Itoro:

Sista Idara, are you almost done? We still have to do my hair.

Idara:

[*stops singing*] Oh yeah, I'm coming, I'm almost done. I'm trying to get this right, you know how the price of food goes up the closer we get to Christmas, I don't want you guys to be stranded in January.

Itoro:

[*teasingly*] Of course not, especially since Ani might finally come for you.
Idara:
[*blushes*] Oh Itoro, stop teasing me. Please let me focus.
Itoro:
But it's true, I heard from Mama Mfon, Mama Ani's sister's brother-in-law's cousin that he should be around sometime before January. Why else would he come back if not to see you?
Idara:
Itoro, you and gossip, you too like *amebo*. You want to be like those market men who gossip from sunup to sundown?
Itoro:
Sista Idara, leave that one abeg. And even if it's gossip, they say there's no smoke without fire. If they're saying he's coming back soon, then it's probably true.
Idara:
[*faking unaffectedness*] Probably…maybe.
Itoro:
Abeg your posing is too much, as if you're not excited to see him too. [*moves closer conspiratorially*] I'm sure he's coming back because he heard that you've passed through the *nkuho* and you're now more beautiful. Before the entire men's folk comes knocking down Papa's door for your hand, he'd want to be first in line to claim his bride.
Idara:
[*blushes in embarrassment but is obviously pleased*] Ohhh Itoro, you're too troublesome. [*Gets a longing look in her eyes*] Of course I'll be happy to see Aniekan, it's been so long. His letters are too

inconsistent, I can't wait to hear how he's been doing all these years.
Itoro:
And of course make his favorite *edikang ikong*, the man would just die from a happy stomach [*ends with a laugh*].
Idara:
[*laughs along*] Ohhhh Itoro, leave me alone dis girl, you like trouble. Anyway, what hairstyle did you want again?
Itoro:
Ehen, now you're talking! [*sits on a stool in front of* Idara, *facing forward*] I want that style that Apena had in Masquerade, that episode we watched last week. The one that her hair came to her shoulders and…
Offstage, Mama Idara *shouts for* Idara.
Mama Idara:
Idara! Idara!! Where are you?
Idara:
[*goes to the corridor to respond*] Mama? I'm with Itoro in the room. What's the problem?
Mama Idara *enters, smiling giddily.*
Mama Idara:
Idara, *adiaha mmi*, they're coming.
Idara:
[*confused*] Ehn? Who's coming where?
Mama Idara:
Who else? Your beloved.
Idara:
[*hopeful*] Aniekan?
Mama Idara:

This girl, do you have more than one? Yes, Aniekan and his family. Mama Ani sent Etim to deliver the news just now.

Itoro:

[*shouts with joy*] Ehhhhhhhh!!!!! *Abasi* has done it *o*. Idara, they're coming. *Abi*, I told you your fat curves would grip him. He could not resist any longer, after all, he's an Efik man!!!!

Mama Idara:

I've already spoken to Papa Idara, he's gone to the call center to inform our kinsmen. I'll have to send Effiong to the market to get the items we need for their visit.

Idara:

[*still in shock*] When?

Mama Idara:

When? When what? Oh! This Saturday, in the morning.

Itoro:

[*surprised*] Whoa! That's 6 days from today.

Mama Idara:

Yes but we'll be ready. We've already waited for 5 yrs, 6 days is nothing.

Itoro:

Idara, they're coming!

Mama Idara:

Didn't I tell you that once you completed the *nkuho* ritual, he'll come running home? *Abi* Itoro? [Itoro *concurs loudly*] Didn't I tell you? [*beats her chest for emphasis*] I, Nsemeke, daughter of Chief Aniefiok, wife of Udeme Inyang, said it that no man born of a woman can resist the *UYAI MBOPO*, the beauty of the fattened girl, and my daughter Idara-abasi is the most beautiful of them all. Ehn [*begins praising Idara in Efik while* Idara *blushes from all the* attention] *Utuenikang mmi*! *Ndoko mma*! *Mbopo mmi*! Idara mi! *Obonghwan mmi*! The one who devoured all her meals in the fattening room without complaint!

Itoro:
[*picks up from* Mama Idara, *gets really animated with her words and descriptions*] *Mkpouto mmi*! *Uyai mbopo*! The fattest of them all! The one who went into the fattening room and came out radiant! The one that makes men stutter when she swings her hips! The one that makes the ground trembles! The amazing *ekombi* dancer, the light-footed stepper! The very picture of an angel! *Abasi*'s special gift to mankind! Didn't I tell you that he was around and was coming for you? Never doubt me, I'm never wrong.

Mama Idara:
[*turns to* Itoro] You, this girl, you've started gossiping again like all those old men at the canteen. Come and help me gather the items, there's so much to do.

Itoro:
[*excited*] Yes, let's go. We need to show him what he has been missing all these years.

Mama Idara *and* Itoro *leave*.

Idara:
[*suddenly remembers*] Itoro, what about your hair?
Realizing she's now alone, she sits on the bed, staring into space, her budgeting task long forgotten.

Idara:
He's coming. [*opens her dresser and picks up an old but clearly cherished picture of* Andy, *stroking her finger over his image*] Aniekan, you're coming.

Lights out, curtain falls.

SCENE 4: EKPANG NKUKWO

Lights on, curtain open.

Narrator:
It's Friday afternoon, and one day before the engagement ceremony with the Inyangs. Idongesit and Mama Ani have prepared *Ekpang Nkukwo*, a traditional Efik dish made with cocoyam and leafy greens, including various proteins and periwinkles. Idongesit goes to call Andy and Angela for lunch but stops by the living room to set the dining table. Etim passes by.

Idongesit:
Etim, we made *ekpang nkukwo* o.

Etim:
[*excited*] Yes! Let me quickly return this DVD to Papa Emem's shop. I'm coming.

Idongesit:
Okay, hurry back [Etim *exits*. Idongesit *continues to* Andy and Angela's *room*] [*under her breath*]. Let's see if they'll end their fast today [*normal voice*]. Bro Ani, Angela, it's time for lunch.

Angela:
Awesome, what would we be having?

Idongesit:
It's called *Ekpang Nkukwo*. It's made from cocoyam and it's very nutritious, with lots of fish and meat inside too.

Angela:
Oh no, I don't think I can eat that. Andy, can we go somewhere to eat, please?

Idongesit:

But you haven't even tried it yet. I know it can be difficult trying new foods but you should try to eat just a little. I promise you, you won't regret it. Ask Bro Ani, he loves *ekpang nkukwo* too.
Andy:
Idongesit. [*turns to* Angela] Are you sure you don't want to try it?
Angela:
Absolutely. If I can't pronounce it, I don't think I want it. And don't try to force me either.
Andy:
[*sighs deeply*] Alright. [*turns to* Idongesit] Tell Mama, we're going out for lunch.
Idongesit:
[*in Efik*] Brother, Mama would not like this at all. At all. This is the 4th time this week that you've refused our food. You guys should at least eat lit...
Mama Ani:
[*shouts from a distance*] Idongesit, what is taking you so long? Where are they?
Idongesit:
Bro Ani, I'm begging you [*glances at* Angela *then whispers to* Andy]. It's not worth it.
Andy:
Idongesit, please leave now.
Idongesit *exhales deeply, then exits.*
All is quiet for a bit. Andy *and* Angela *go out to the courtyard, getting ready to leave. They don't notice* Mama Ani, *standing in the corner.*
Mama Ani:
Idongesit said you're not staying for lunch.
Angela:

Yeah we're going out to eat.

Mama Ani:
But I've already cooked.

Angela:
Yeah I'm sorry, Andy and I can't eat the food. Too smelly and mushy.

A brief silence ensues.

Mama Ani:
[*speaks to* Angela *but looks at* Andy] I need to speak to Aniekan alone.

Angela:
[*stares at the two of them*] Okay, I'll be inside Andy.

Angela *exits.* Mama Ani *and* Andy *remain in silence for a bit.*

Mama Ani:
Idongesit said you people are not hungry, is that true?

Andy:
Yes and no. We're just going out for a bit, just a little sightseeing, to show Angela around.

Mama Ani:
Okay. So should I keep the food for you two to eat when you get back?

Andy:
No, we'll eat outside. Mama, you know Angela can't eat all these local dishes, why do you keep preparing them?

Mama Ani:
First of all, I don't know because you didn't tell me you were bringing someone to my house [Andy *looks guilty*]. Second, before you people start saying "Mama is wicked", didn't I prepare jollof rice and chicken two days ago and still met her plate half-full?

What was the matter then? Even Queen Elizabeth has eaten jollof rice before.

Andy:
Yes but Angela can't eat spicy food. Or rice. She's very picky in general, trying to watch her weight, you know. I don't want to upset her.

Mama Ani:
So instead you upset me?

Uncle Okon *walks in, oblivious to the tension between mother and son.*

Uncle Okon:
Mesiere o!

Andy:
[*greets him*] *Mesiere* Uncle.

Uncle Okon:
Ani, *idem fo?* Mama Ani, is there food?

Mama Ani:
[*still looking at* Andy] *Ekpang nkukwo*. Idongesit is inside.

Uncle Okon:
[*clearly happy*] Very good, God would bless you Mama Ani [*goes inside*] Idongesit!

A brief silence ensues.

Mama Ani:
Aniekan, have you finalized the arrangements to see Idara's people tomorrow? You've been going out a lot but I haven't seen you buy anything for the ceremony yet.

Andy:
[*looking very uneasy now*] No, I haven't had the time yet...

Mama Ani:

You've had 5 days. In fact, you've had 5 years. When are you going to find the time?

Andy:

Mama, I've been meaning to tell you [*exhales deeply*]... I'm not going to marry her.

Mama Ani:

[*quiet for a bit*] Hmm...okay, we can postpone it a bit. Maybe January, that's not too far...

Andy:

[*interrupts her, exasperated*] No Mama, I'm not going to marry her. Ever.

A brief silence ensues.

Mama Ani:

Aniekan, this is not the time for games, I'm not smiling with you.

Andy:

Mama, I'm serious.

Mama Ani:

[*voice slightly raised*] What do you mean you won't marry her? Idaraabasi that you were chasing around like an egret to cattle since you were a small boy? Idaraabasi, the accomplished accountant with a Master's degree and a car? Idaraabasi, whom YOU [*points at his chest*] gave your word to marry, promising her of the family you two would build together when you came back from America?

Andy:

Mama, you're not looking at this right...

Mama Ani:

Not looking at this right? Wait, I'm coming, stay here [*goes inside and comes back quickly with a photo of* Idara *at her emerging ceremony, all dressed up*]. Look, [*pushes photo into* Andy's *view*] take a look at your bride, the most beautiful woman to emerge from the fattening room this season. If only you were here to see the men swarming at Inyang's compound to ask for his daughter's hand, you wouldn't be talking rubbish like this. Look at how beautiful and fat she has become!

Andy:
[*raises voice*] But Mama, that's the problem. She's FAT!

Mama Ani:
[*calmly*] Ehen and what's the problem? Instead of you to be thanking God that your bride gained weight. Not every girl who passes through the *nkuho* is so blessed. I had to stay for 5 extra weeks because I wasn't putting on enough weight.

Andy:
[*emphatically*] I don't want a fat bride. I don't want a fat wife.

Mama Ani:
[*raises voice*] What do you mean you don't want a fat wife? For generations, even before the white man came to our ports, the Ntia family sent their daughters to the *nkuho* and MARRIED women who emerged from the fattening room. I, Nsemeke Ntia, passed through the fattening room before your late father, God rest his soul, came to ask for my hand and I gave him 4 [*holds up 4 fingers*] good children before *Abasi* took him and Akpan your older brother. Your sister, Idongesit, would pass through the *nkuho* before going to her husband's house. So please tell me, what is wrong with being fat? Except if you're saying something is wrong with us? [*points fingers at herself*] Wrong with me?

Andy:

[*hurriedly*] Mama, I never said anything is wrong with you or our family. I'm just saying what I want and don't want, that's all.
A brief silence ensues.
Mama Ani:
[*calmly*] Okay. *Oya*, tell me, what do you want?
Andy:
Mama, I'm going to marry Angela.
Mama Ani:
[*dramatically throws her fingers behind her back and clicks them to ward off Andy's statement*]. *Abasi ikana*, God forbid! Over my dead body! The ground would swallow me before I allow it! The locusts would eat out my eyes before you marry that girl! *Abasi* would take me to your father and my first son before that happens!!!
Andy:
[*exasperated*] Mama…
Mama Ani:
Aniekan, I don't understand you. You've always liked smart, intelligent girls with flesh. That's why you liked Idara in the first place, because she had body and she challenged you mentally. Or am I lying? Now you're telling me that you want to marry this unemployed girl that harmattan wind would blow away like a leaf. What is the problem? What changed?!
Andy:
Mama, this fattening tradition is old-school and outdated. I want a beautiful wife. I deserve a beautiful bride. And that is Angela. Anywhere I go in America, anywhere I go in the world, I'll be respected because she's on my arm. Slim, not too much fat or bum-bum, just perfect.
Mama Ani:

[*calmly*] Idara is beautiful.
Andy:
No, she's fat.
Mama Ani:
[*without pause*] Fat is beautiful.
Andy:
[*retorts quickly*] No it's not. Fat is NOT beautiful, Mama. If I go anywhere in America, anywhere in the world *sef*, with Idara, people would look down on me, they'll call me the man with the fat wife, the man with the UGLY wife! That my wife can beat me up, that she can swallow me whole! It might have been good for Papa, and our ancestors but it's certainly not good for me [*shakes his head vigorously*]. Mama you want me to have a beautiful bride right? That's Angela. Tall, slim, she's perfect. If she's good for the white man, then she's good enough for me.
Mama Ani:
[*calmly*] Aniekan, stop these games. Idara is your bride. Her people would be waiting for us tomorrow morning and as surely as I gave birth to you, we're going.
Andy:
[*retorts*] No Mama, I'm not.
Angela *appears in the courtyard and interrupts at that very moment.*
Angela:
Andy, are you guys done now? I'm starving...
Mama Ani:
[*charges for* Angela, *screaming now*] His name is ANIEKAN!!!! I named him Aniekanabasi after my father and his father, the great hunter of Creek Town!!!!! [Andy *moves to shield* Angela *from* Mama Ani's *wrath while* Idongesit *and* Uncle Okon *rush outside*]

Aniekanabasi meaning "who is greater than God"!!! [*Uncle Okon is pulling her away now bu*t Mama Ani's *clearly strong*] Not ANDY, HE'S NOT YOUR ANDY!!! [*turns to* Andy] Teach her your name, the one I gave you. Teach her your culture, who you are, and our customs. [*speaking to* Angela *now*] If you cannot accept us, then leave us alone! LEAVE, GO AWAY!!! [*by now,* Angela *and* Idongesit *are crying*].

Uncle Okon:

[*almost carrying her now*] Mama Ani, Nsemeke, control yourself now. [*turns to* Andy] What did you say to annoy your Mama?

Mama Ani:

[*still shouting*] You will marry Idara *o*! I'm not hearing any foolish nonsense explanation! You will go to the Inyang house and you'll ask for her hand officially! You will settle this matter once and for all!

Andy:

No I would not. Mama, please listen.

Angela:

[*same time as* Andy] Who's Idara?

Mama Ani:

[*surprised at* Angela's *question*] You wicked boy, you haven't told her that you're engaged?! [*stops* Andy *as he tries to reply. Shrugs out of* Uncle Okon's *hold but remains in her spot*] [*calmer*] NO. No, I have listened to you enough. For 5 years, I have smiled and made excuses as people have asked why you refused to finish what you started. "Oh he's busy in America", "oh he's gathering money for the wedding", "he's building a house for them", excuses, LIES!!! For 5 years, I have defended you. That ends TODAY [*points to the ground to emphasize her point*]. You would marry Idara, the woman who has waited for you diligently, your beautiful AND FAT bride. Or you won't marry anyone, pick one.

Andy:

Mama don't be impossible, I'm not a child.

Mama Ani:

[*quiet for a bit*] [*calmly*] No, you're not, you're a man now. And that's why you would handle this matter yourself. Go ahead and disappoint Idara and the Inyangs. Go ahead and go back on your word. You [*pointing to* Andy] would take the shame on your own head [*points to his head*]. I, [*does a handwashing motion*] I am washing my hands off this matter [*starts heading inside then stops and turns around*]. And if you're leaving this house, please don't bother coming back [*in the background* Idongesit *cries* "Ah! Mama"]. God knows you've stayed away long enough [*turns and goes inside*].

Uncle Okon:

[*frantic*] Wait, Mama Ani. *Nsi tipe?* [*turns to* Andy *and* Angela] Go for now, let me talk to her, she doesn't want to see you.

Andy:

[*calmly to* Angela] Let's go.

Andy *and* Angela *exit.*

Idongesit:

Mama, please wait.

Uncle Okon *and* Idongesit *exit, following* Mama Ani.

Etim *enters and makes a beeline for the living room. He sees the serving dish on the table and his eyes widen with glee. He lifts the lid to discover all the food's gone.*

Etim:

[*confused, he shouts*] Ahnahn, what happened to all the *ekpang nkukwo*?!

Idongesit [*offstage, shouts back*]: SHUT UP ETIM!!!
Curtain falls, and lights dim

SCENE 5: SAÑA SUÑ
Narrator:
Three weeks have now passed since Mama Ani and Andy's big fight. Andy has sent word to the Inyangs that he wouldn't be coming for Idara, severing ties with the family. News has spread across town and his decision has been denounced by everyone, including his family.
Lights brighten, curtain lifts, We see Idara, Itoro, *and* Mama Idara *sitting in the living room, looking sullen as they listen to the radio.*

Narrator:
Upon Andy's rejection, Idara is devastated but tries to hide her grief. Her cheeks are puffier than usual, a tell-tale sign that she's been overeating to cope with her disappointment.
Radio blasts Fela's *Lady*.
[*Radio:* "If you call am woman African woman no go 'gree; She go say, she go say, "I be lady, oh', She go say, "I be lady, oh""]

Idara:
[*stands up suddenly*] I'm going out.

Mama Idara:
Ahan where?

Idara:
[*scrambles for an answer*] We need eggs, I forgot to put it on our list.

Itoro:
But I bought eggs yester... [*trails off,* Idara *is already gone*].

Mama Idara:
[*to* Itoro] My dear, leave her, it's okay.

Aside, we see Andy *and* Angela *sitting in their room.* Angela *is searching in her luggage for something.*

Angela:
Arghhhhh!

Andy:
What? Did you hurt yourself?

Angela:
No, I just realized I'm out of sanitary pads and I'm about to start.

Andy:
[*confused*] Oh? [*realization dawns*] Ohhhh.

Angela:
Yes. Do you think I could ask Idongesit to help me?

Andy:
[*quickly*] No, no, no, no. I'll go.

Angela:
You're sure?

Andy:
Yes. See you in a bit [*exits*].

Lights dim and brighten again. Now we see Idara *walking on a path. She comes to a fork in the road. She goes left and suddenly comes upon* Andy *who hasn't noticed her yet.*

Idara:
[*calmly*] Ani.

Andy:
[*initially confused but quickly recognizes her*] Idara.
A brief silence ensues.

Idara:

Ikut enyin. How're you doing?
Andy:
I'm doing well, you? How's Mama and Papa?
Idara:
[*initially quiet*] They're as well as they can manage. Papa had a bit of a shock when you didn't…[*stops herself*] but he's doing alright now, he's playing drafts at Papa Imoh's house. Mama…well, Mama is Mama [*forces a smile*].
Andy:
[*looks embarrassed, shakes the back of his neck*] Idara… [*trails off*].
Idara:
[*interrupts*] I should have known.
Andy:
[*confused*] What?
Idara:
I should have known that you weren't coming back for me. From staying in America for 5 good years to the lack of letters or updates, the writing was on the wall. I should have known.
Andy:
Idara…[he trails off]
Idara:
[*seeing he won't give an explanation, she continues*] I've seen you around with her, you know, the lady. I can understand staying in America as long as you did. You're ambitious, and so am I, that was part of the attraction. I can understand falling in love with another woman, I mean, these things happen, 5 years is a long time. What I don't get is WHY? [*close to tears now*] Why not me? And why string me along for so long? You sent Godii and Uncle Okon to

break off the engagement. You didn't even have the decency to show your face before my Papa.

Andy:
[*hurriedly*] Idara, Idara, I'm sorry but I just couldn't go through with it. When it came down to it, Angela was the one, please try to understand. It wasn't anything serious at first but she made me laugh and I was captivated by her beauty.

Idara:
[*interrupts*] Her beauty? You thought I was beautiful! You used to talk about when I'll go into the *ufok nkuho* and come out fat and be even more beautiful for you, making you the envy of your peers. [*grabs her breasts and buttocks*] These breasts, this *yansh*, [*grabs her stomach*] this stomach, used to get you all excited. What changed?

Andy:
[*embarrassed and clearly unsure of himself*] I don't know, it's just not my preference anymore.

A brief silence ensues.

Idara:
Is she from a wealthy family?

Andy:
No, not exactly…

Idara:
Is this for a Green card?

Andy:
[*visibly shocked*] No Idara, what do you think of me?

Idara:
[*ignores his comment, keeps going with a break*] Is she an engineer like you?

Andy:
Angela? [*chortles*] Not at all, she hates math.
Idara:
Did you go to university together?
Andy:
Oh no, Angela's not the school type. She loves fashion, hair, and animals. Stuff like that. She's very good with them though, she's trying to get into modeling these days.
Idara:
[*eyes widen like she's just had a eureka moment*] Oh I see.
Andy:
What? See what?
Idara:
You've become one of them.
Andy:
What? One of them? [*looks around him, confused*] Who's them?
Idara:
Lepa chasers. Boys who run after slim girls because the West says they're the finest now.
Andy:
[*stunned into silence, stutters*] Uh…no…huh.
Idara:
Am I lying?
Andy:
Idara…
Idara:
Does she eat our local food?
Andy:

No, Angela loves to watch her weight. The other day, she refused to try *Edikang Ikong*.
Idara:
But Edikang Ikong is your favorite.
A brief silence ensues. Idara *exhales deeply.*
Idara:
[*slightly pained*] Do you love her? Does she make you truly happy?
Andy:
Well…yes, I mean…[*trails off*].
Idara:
[*corks her head in observation*] You don't even know.
A brief silence ensues.
Idara:
[*exhales deeply*] Thank you Aniekan.
Andy:
What? What for?
Idara:
Thank you for breaking off the engagement. You've wounded me deeply, even embarrassed me, and oh, Mama, Papa, and our kinsmen were obviously offended. I'm sure we're the current gossip and laughingstock in town. But they'll get over it, Mama and Papa, everybody, we will. However, if you'd come to complete the wedding arrangements, sooner or later, I would have come to know your true feelings and I'd have never gotten over the fact that I married a man who no longer found me attractive, who thinks being fat has made me ugly. [*exhales again*] So thank you again. You've spared me from a lifetime of feeling inferior and unworthy of you. I'd have been soooooo miserable. But

thankfully, you didn't come so I don't have to live in misery. However, you Aniekan [*gestures to* Andy], you're already there.

Andy:

[*confused*] How am I miserable? Idara, stop speaking in riddles.

Idara:

[*in a clear voice*] You're miserable because you say you want something, but you only want it because you've been told that that's what you should want. You're willing to throw US away, and our local customs away because the white man says that fat is ugly and slim is the best. Well, [*laughs to herself, looks upward, and raises her hands*], thank *Abasi* I'm fat now so I don't have to deal with what you've become for the rest of my life.

Andy is stunned, frozen on the spot.

Idara:

[*genuinely smiling now*] *Saña suñ* Aniekan. I still wish you all the best, although I hope we never meet again [*turns for the right fork of the path*].

Andy:

[*utterly confused*] *Saña suñ*? But I'm not traveling anytime soon.

Idara:

[*turns around*] *Saña suñ* Aniekan. A mirage is a journey too. [*Gestures to the sanitary pad in his hand*]. And you have the wrong size, she'll bleed right through. Go back and ask for the biggest size. It doesn't cost more than 50 naira, so don't let Mama Boniface cheat you. *Saña suñ* Aniekan. [*turns around and leaves, exits stage*].

Andy *remains frozen on the spot, staring in her wake. He soon recovers and raises the pack of sanitary pads in his hand.*

Andy:

[*whispers to himself*] Biggest size…

Turns back in the direction he came but keeps looking back wistfully. Exits.
THE END

Domestic Violence in Contemporary Nigerian Drama: A Discourse of Julie Okoh's *In Our Own Voices*

Eziwho Emenike AZUNWO

Abstract

The study examines the issue of domestic violence in contemporary Nigerian drama with a particular focus on Julie Okoh's *In Our Own Voices*. Upon the sad reality that many women in the 21st century still suffer from one form of violence or another with their perpetrators going scot free from the law necessitates the motivation for the study. The study is predominantly literary in methodology as it relied mainly on Okoh's *In Our Own Voices* as the primary source of data. The findings of the study include that most Nigerian men hide under the cloak of patriarchal tradition to unleash violence on women. The study also finds that the high level of corruption in the Nigerian judicial system constitutes one of the reasons why perpetrators of violence against women are not served their due punishment. It is based on the foregoing that the study recommends the need for the traditional societies in Nigeria to review their cultural values with the view to expunge traditions that infringe on human rights. The study also canvasses on the need for a transparent and working judicial system in Nigeria.

Introduction

Categorically a phenomenon, domestic violence is a type of abuse perpetrated by one person against another in a domestic setting such as in marriage or cohabitation. Often times, when people think of domestic abuse, they make the mistake of equating it to domestic violence. However, domestic abuse is a broader concept, includes any attempt by one person in an intimate relationship or marriage to dominate and control the other. Be that as it may, the converging point is that domestic violence and abuse are used for one purpose and one purpose only; to gain and maintain total control over another. It has been observed that the domestic abuser uses fear, guilt, shame, and intimidation to wear the abuse to down-keep him/her under his/her thumb. It is important to state in clear terms that domestic violence and abuse can happen to anyone; it does not discriminate. Hence, it occurs within all age ranges, ethnic backgrounds, and economic levels. And while women are more often victimized, men also experience abuse especially verbal and emotional. Scholars of gender studies such as Roxanne Dryden-Edwards and Melissa Conrad Stoppler have identified many signs of abusive relationships with the fear of one's partner as the most telling.

Available accounts in gender studies also reveal that one of the key manifestations of social change in contemporary Africa especially Nigeria is the progressive increase in the participation of married women in the paid labour industry. Relatively, scholars of gender studies such as Mary Wollenstonecraft and Helen Showalter observe that women that are high in marital dependency have or perceive few viable alternatives to marriage, which force them to be more tolerant of negative treatment from their husbands, including physical abuse. They also observe that women who have children and rely on their husbands for financial support cannot easily leave abusive marriages, nor do they possess sufficient resources to negotiate changes in their husbands' behaviour. Based on the observations so far, it becomes unequivocal to say that marital dependency traps women in abusive marriages. Importantly also, researchers on family violence observe that persons who occupy low positions within the economic structure are more likely to use violence. Against this background, Macmillan and Gartner assert that "diminished resources lead to stress, frustration and conflict that can culminate in violence between spouses. Resource deprivation that accompanies unemployment should thus increase risk of spousal violence" (948). Similarly, domestic violence can be physical or psychological, and it can affect anyone of any age, gender, race or sexual orientation. It may include behaviours meant to scare, physically harm, or control a partner. While every relationship is different, domestic violence generally involves an unequal power dynamic in which one partner tries to assert control over the other in a variety of ways. Against this background, this study shall attempt an examination of the issue of domestic violence raised in Julie Okoh's *In Our Own Voices*.

Theoretical Framework
The theoretical framework of this study is anchored on Lenore Walker's theory of Cycle of Violence. This theory is divided into three distinct phases which are repeated over and over again in the

abusive relation. As a result, domestic violence and/or abuse rarely involves a single isolated incident of violence. Rather, the abuse becomes a repetitive pattern in the relationship. According to Walker, the first stage in the cycle of violence is tension building. During the tension building stage, the victim is often subjected to less serious nonviolent forms of abuse such as threats and insults. Victims soon come to realize that the verbal threats usually precede physical violence and will therefore attempt to delay its onset. For example, the victim may act compliant in the hope of mollifying the batterer and avoiding a violent outburst, but eventually the inevitable occurs; the physical assault. The second stage in the cycle of violence is acute battering. The acute battering stage is marked by uncontrolled physical aggression, which may be extremely violent in nature. It is during the acute-battering stage that victims are most likely to sustain injuries ranging from bruises, cuts, broken bones, disfigurement and miscarriage to loss of life. The acute battering, however, tends to be abrupt as the violence usually lasts only a few minutes. Immediately following an acute battering incident, the abuser usually acts remorseful.

Walker describes the third stage in the cycle of violence theory as loving and contrite, or the "honeymoon" stage. The batterer is apologetic as well as attentive to the victim. The abuser may shower the victim with gifts, compliments and sincere promises that it will never happen again. The victim becomes reassured that the perpetrator loves her and that the relationship can be salvaged. The victim may actually begin to feel responsible for the violent outburst. Predictably, the stage ends, tension building resumes and the cycle of violence persists.

The Concept of Feminism

Since its emergence as a distinct area of literary discourse, the term feminism has been subjected to a wide range of definitions. Interestingly, these definitions are often drawn from a perspective, be it political, economic or cultural. Of all the definitions of feminism, the commonest is that which associates it with 'struggle'. However, it is pertinent to mention here that feminism transcends the term struggle. It is fundamentally "a collective term or systems of belief and theories that pay special attention to women's rights and women's position in culture and society" (Okoh 7). For Quayson, feminism has been about challenging the representations of women and arguing for better conditions for them (586). In Quayson's analogy, the term representation has two meanings, both of which are relevant to post-colonialism and to feminism. The first and more political one has to do with the matter of political representation, something which even in a democracy arguably never fully satisfies the needs and aspirations of all the people for whom democratic systems are set up. Against this backdrop, Quayson argues that "For political representation to be fully representative, it has to be constantly reviewed by those it claims to serve" (586). The second and no less significant definition lies in the area of the discursive, in the ways in which metaphors, tropes and concepts are used to project an image of some person or persons. Quayson notes that:

> Discursive representation has serious effects the lived domain of everyday life and crucially sets up forms of potential agency which are offered as a means of defining subject positions in the world. Both political and discursive

dimensions of representations are relevant to feminism and post-colonialism, with the two frequently being conflated in general discussions so that the discursive representation of Third World women is often seen as untimely of political consequence (586).

For Haralambos and Holborn, the development of feminism has led to attention being focused on the subordinate position of women in many societies (103). They argue that feminist sociologists have been mainly responsible for developing theories of gender inequality, yet there is little agreement about the causes of this inequality and on about what actions should be taken to reduce or end it.

Drama and Feminism
The issue of feminism has been a recurring decimal in both Western and Nigerian drama. From the classical dramas of Euripedes, Sophocles and Aristophanes, the issue of feminism have been a visible subject in drama. As a matter of fact, the most prominent reflection of feminism envisioned in the classical era is that portrayed by Aristophanes in *Lysistrata* where the women of Athens and Sparta unite and embark on a sex strike in order to compel their husbands to end the Peloponnesian war. Interestingly, Aristophanes' play has inspired a handful of plays with similar plot. One of such plays is J.P. Clark's *The Wives Revolt* and later, Barclays Ayakoroma's *Dance on His Grave*. Drawing from the Aristophanes' model, these plays portray the agitation and struggle by the women for equal or fair treatment by their male counterparts who function as their husbands and fathers. In both plays i.e. *The Wives Revolt* and

Dance on His Grave, the women drawn from various Niger Delta communities, resort to sex strike and decline from domestic chores as they embark on a self- imposed exile as a way of registering their protest over the denial of their self- worth by the men. Julie Okoh takes a similar cue from Aristophanes in the crafting of her masterpiece *Edewede* where the heroine of the play mobilizes the women in her community and embarks on exile as a way of protesting against female genital mutilation. Like the victories recorded in Aristophanes *Lysistrata*, Clark's *Wives Revolt* and Ayakoroma's *Dance on His Grave*, in Okoh's *Edewede*, women succeed in their protest as the King abolishes the practice of female circumcision in the community.

Similarly, Okoh's *Closed Doors*, is yet another play with a feminist undertone. The women in the play lament that wherever they go "doors" of opportunities are closed against them, they face sexual harassment from their bosses in the office and when they do not oblige to their erotic cravings, they face the threat of losing their jobs despite their years of labour, acquiring a degree in the university. In the case of Bola, a character in the play and a graduate, she is a victim of sexual harassment by her boss and loses her job on account of her insistence in terminating the pregnancy which her boss desperately desires to keep. Just as Bola, other characters in the play suffer similar fate. Eki for instance who also is a victim of rape takes to prostitution meanwhile, Belema, Amina and Tracy are all victims of sexual confinement and they seek sexual freedom because the same men who abuse them at will, end up closing doors of opportunities and economic liberation against them. Okoh's choice of floating female characters throughout the play except for the character of the policemen is an intentional dramatic style to classify the play as a feminist play.

Be that as it may, Zulu Sofola departs radically from the view of Okoh in her play *Wizard of Law* where the latter portrays women as gold diggers. This outlook is reflected boldly through the character of Sikira, the wife of Romoni, the lawyer. Sikira is a stereotype of the modern woman to be found in most Nigerian cities. This type of woman often does not believe in marriage as a sanctimonious institution between two people. Such women go into marriage solely for economic gains. Citing Sikira;

> That was how he talked big twenty years ago when he came to marry me. I thought he had something so I agreed to be his wife. I married him and refused the hands of Mamud and Adamu because I thought he was shaking money in his pocket (52).

What is most striking in the above statement is the materialistic streak in Sikira. Obviously, love which should be a major ingredient in marriage is glaringly absent in Sikira's matrimonial life. Her passion for money and fancy clothes makes her resist the urge of showing affection nor care for Romoni. Sofola however, uses Sikira to comment on a popular trend found in most Nigerian big cities. Such women are very exploitative and do not bother to hide it. These modern breed of materialistic and exploitative young women is a contrast to what is obtained in Sofola's image of the traditional women as reflected in the depth of Ogwoma's love in *Wedlock of the Gods*.

It is note-worthy that women like Sirika make themselves vulnerable to men's derision. In this vein, Mary Wollstonecraft admonishes that woman should eradicate the intellect that makes them believe that their major duty is to serve men. She puts it thus: "confined in a cage like the birds they have nothing to do than to plum themselves…to the desire of establishing…the only way women can rise in the world is by marriage" (75). This is to say that women who bears only cheap virtue think that they can become high in the society by attracting a man. This she said is tantamount to prostitution because to this instance, women are subject to slavery by their sensibility. Outside the dramaturgy of Julie Okoh, the subject of feminism has gained prominence in Nigerian drama with a handful of feminist playwrights who remains consistent in their portrayal of the feminist vision in their works. Such playwrights include: Stella Oyedepo, Irene Salami, Tracy Chima Utoh- Ezeajugh and Osita Ezenwanebe among others.

Domestic Violence: A Global Outlook
The term domestic violence has been subjected to series of definition and interpretation by scholars of sociology and gender studies. It has been described to include behaviours meant to scare, physically harm, or control a partner. History has it that the first known use of the term domestic violence was in an address to the Parliament of the United Kingdom by Jack Ashley in 1973 (*National Women's Aid Federation*). The term previously referred primarily to civil unrest, violence from within a country as opposed to violence perpetrated by a foreign power. Traditionally, domestic violence was mostly associated with physical violence. Terms such as wife

abuse, wife beating and wife battering were used, but have declined in popularity due to efforts to include unmarried partners etc.

Domestic violence does not discriminate. Anyone of any age, race, sexual orientation, religion gender can be a victim or perpetrator of domestic violence. It can happen to people who are married, living together or who are dating. It affects people of all socioeconomic backgrounds and education levels. According to the *National Domestic Violence Hotline*:

> Domestic violence includes behaviors that physically harm, arouse fear, prevent a partner from doing what they wish or force them to behave in ways they do not want. It includes the use of physical and sexual violence, threats and intimidation, emotional abuse and economic deprivation. Many of these different forms of domestic violence/abuse can be occurring at any one time within the same intimate relationship.

It has been observed that it is not always easy to tell at the beginning of a relationship if it will become abusive. This is largely because many abusive partners may seem absolutely perfect in the early stages of a relationship. Possessive and controlling behaviours do not always appear overnight, rather, emerge and intensify as the relationship grows (*National Domestic Violence Hotline*). It has also been noted that domestic violence does not look the same in every relationship because every relationship is different. But one thing most abusive relationships have in common is that the abusive partner does many different kinds of things to have more power and control over their partner. The *National Domestic Violence Hotline*

enumerated some of the signs of an abusive relationship to include a partner who;
- Tells you that you can never do anything right
- Shows extreme jealousy of your friends and time spent away
- Keeps you or discourages you from seeing friends or family members
- Insults, demeans or shames you with put-downs
- Controls every penny spent in the household
- Takes your money or refuses to give you money for necessary expenses
- Looks at you or acts in ways that scare you
- Controls who you see, where you go or what you do
- Prevents you from making your own decisions
- Tells you that you are a bad parent or threatens to harm or take away your children
- Prevents you from working or attending school
- Destroys your property or threatens to hurt or kill your pets
- Intimidates you with guns, knives or other weapons
- Pressures you to have sex when you do not want to or do things sexually you are not comfortable with
- Pressures you to use drugs or alcohol

Similarly, Fareo Oluremi quoting *National Network to End Domestic Violence* informs that domestic violence and abuse is not limited to obvious physical violence but includes endangerment, criminal coercion, kidnapping, unlawful imprisonment, trespassing, harassment and stalking (2). The *UNICEF Report* of 2005 corroborates the submission of The *National Domestic Violence Hotline* that domestic violence is a global phenomenon and also that families from all social, racial, economic, educational and religious backgrounds experience domestic violence in different ways. In the United States of America, each year, women experience about 4.8 million intimate partner related physical assaults and rapes while men are victims of about 2.9 million partner related physical assaults.

In parts of the third world generally and in West Africa particularly, domestic violence is prevalent and reportedly justified and condoned in some cultures. For instance, 56 percent of Indian women surveyed by an agency justified that wife-beating on grounds like – bad cook, disrespectful to in-laws, producing more girls and leaving home without informing among others (*UNICEF Report*).

History has it that in most legal systems around the world, domestic violence has been addressed only from the 1990s onwards. Indeed, before the late 20th century, in most countries there was very little protection in law or in practice against it. In 1993, the United Nations published a document titled "Strategies for Confronting Domestic Violence: A Resource Manual". This publication urged countries around the world to treat domestic violence as a criminal act as well as stated that the right to private family life does not include the right to abuse family members, and also acknowledged that, at the time of its writing, most legal systems considered domestic violence to be largely outside the scope of the law, describing the situation at that time as follows; " Physical discipline of children is allowed and, indeed, encouraged in many legal systems and a large number of countries allow moderate physical chastisement of a wife or, if they do not do so now, have done so within the last hundred years. The World Health Organization report titled *Gender, Equity, Human Rights: Gender Based Violence* note that in recent decades, there has been a call for the end of legal impunity for domestic violence- impunity often based on the idea that such acts as private and that the Istanbul Convention is the first legally binding instrument in Europe dealing with domestic violence and violence against women.

It is also pertinent to inform that laws on domestic violence vary from country to country. While it is generally accepted in the Western world, this is not the case in many developing countries. For instance, in 2010, the United Arab Emirates Supreme Court ruled that a man has the right to physically discipline his wife and children as long as long he does not leave physical marks (172). The social responsibility of domestic violence also differs from country to country. Whereas, in most developed countries domestic violence is considered unacceptable by most people, in many regions of the world, the views are different. It has been observed also that violence against women tends to be less prevalent in developed Western nations, and more normalized in the developing world (Felson, 21).

Domestic Violence in Nigeria

The issue of domestic violence has become rampant in contemporary Nigeria. This is largely because there has not been serious judicial mechanism set in motion to arrest and prosecute the perpetrators of this menace. In a pilot study on the abuse of women in the family carried out by Project Alert, a non-governmental

Organization (NGO) based in Lagos, it was gathered that of the forty-eight (48) women, sixty-four percent (64%) revealed that they have been beaten by their partners while fifty-six (56%) percent of the forty-eight (48) admitted that they have encountered violence by the hands of their male partners. Comparable interviews completed in Oyo State and other parts of Nigeria revealed that parallel results. Similarly, Sylvester Obi and Christopher Ozurumba, in a review of the variables related with aggressive behaviour at home in South East, Nigeria, inform that seventy percent (70%) of respondents reported abuse in their family with ninety-two percent (92%) of the casualties being female and the remaining eight percent being male. Abiodun Fawole and Abike Fawole also carried out an investigation on the degree of the issue of abusive behaviour at home among the civil servants working in the Oyo State Government Service. Fawole et al. inform that ninety-one percent (91%) had been beaten by their partners while forty-four (44%) (i.e. twenty-three percent) women had been beaten. Among the married men, the prevalence of beating was thirty-five percent (35%) while among the married women prevalence was fourteen percent (14%) (62).

The reasons for violent behaviour at home against Nigerian women have been a controversial issue for decades. Different theoretical frameworks proposed by social scientists have not given adequate explanation for this problem. However, it has been observed by social scientists that the brutality against women is connected to some variables namely; behavioural issues, low financial status of men and women, age, women's attitude of women to violence against them, gender norms and childlessness.

In his research on the abusive behaviour at home in Zangon Kataf and Kaura Local Government Areas in Kaduna State, where the consumption of alcohol featured prominently, Yusuf informs that "...the children expressed the view that their fathers divert money meant for their school fees to alcohol consumption" (139). Similarly, a study by Oladipo, Yusuf and Arulugun, shows that of all the causes of physical violence, behavioural factors of partners were found to greatly influence domestic violence against females. According to Oladipo et al., "...females who had partners that drink alcohol experienced sexual violence more than those whose partners do not drink alcohol" (85). Another study conducted by Owoaje and Alaolorun reveals high incidence of physical intimate partner violence in Nigeria. According to Owoaje and Alaolorun; Women at the great risk of physical IPV in this study were those who had experienced psychological or sexual abuse, had attitudes supportive of IPV and those whose partners frequently consumed alcohol (51).

This is in corroboration with the findings of Gelles that;
Marital rape does not occur in isolation ...it tends to occur along with other acts of marital violence. Researchers consistently report that women who experience marital rape are also victims of physical violence (77).

Onigboji, Kofoworola and Onigboji, in their study on married women in urban communities in Lagos State, reveal that alcohol abuse of the male partners, among other variables, make women susceptible to physical abuse. Early scholarship on violence against wives in Nigeria emphasized the role of stress in its entirety. From this point of view, it has been observed that diminished resources can lead to stress, frustration and conflict that may culminate in violence between spouses. Haruna Yusuf observes that "when a woman depends on her husband and asks for money when it is not readily available, she also gets battered" (140). Interestingly, numerous studies that have been carried out in Nigeria show that low educational status of both men and women plays a crucial role in battering. Balogun Akinola, after an exhaustive interview on women working in the business sector and different work environments (i.e. girls in schools and colleges in Lagos State), uncovers that "the respondents whose husbands had tertiary education reported least of battering, while those women whose husbands had no formal education formed the largest population of battered women" (125).

Ndubuisi Ezegbe, Ikechukwu Anyanwu, Esther Onyeoku and Golden Abiogu conducted a study with men on the causes of wife battering in two states in the South Eastern region of Nigeria, Ebonyi and Anambra States respectively. Although the opinion of the respondents on wife battering vary as consequently, they have diverse reasons for such acts, they share a common view that illiteracy on the part of the wife is a cause of battering. This finding is consistent with Akinola's study which shows that the low educational status of the female respondents had influence on physical IPV. According to Akinola "those women with no formal education and those with primary education recorded the highest percentage of battering while those with tertiary education had only sixteen cases" (125).

In a related study carried out by Onigbogi et al., it was revealed that "women with primary education or less education faced an elevated risk of physical violence" (98) The connection between educational status and violence in this study is significant and in line with the findings of Ola Odujirin citing Gelles who stated that physical abuse by woman's partner is inversely related to the woman's educational status. Past research endeavours have shown that the social context of domestic violence is entrenched in the traditional African patriarchal society, where gender roles are assigned to man and woman based on their sexes. Okemgbo et al observe that sexual violence/rape against wives is embedded in the male ideology, where the husband will abuse his wife where something is not done to his satisfaction. Okemgbo et al inform that "About twenty-one percent of the respondents surveyed reported having ever been forced to have sexual intercourse against their will and this happened most between the ages 15-49 (231).

Domestic violence against women is a risk factor for a variety of physical and mental ill health of women. The achievements of women are not only inhibited by the injuries of physical attacks but domestic violence is an implicit threat to social development. Esere et al. assert that;

> By subjecting the woman to rape/violence and without a social structure that endeavours to stop this practice, the women could be made to believe that they are actually inferior to their male counterparts...This can affect their self-image and perception of men in general (2).

The thrust of this segment of review has been to document the various shades and experiences of domestic violence that are peculiar to certain cultures and civilizations.

In Our Own Voices: a Contextual Analysis

Synopsis of *In Our Own Voices*

Okoh's *In Our Own Voices* is an extension of her lamentation over the inhuman and tortuous treatment meted on women by their male counterpart in the name of patriarchy. Through the dramatic form dance, which she calls "Choreodrama", Okoh attempts a cataloguing of the various shades of ill treatment which women experience by the hands of their supposed husbands and spouses. The play harps on such thorny and gender sensitive issues as domestic violence, widow inheritance, forced marriage, commodification of women, childlessness and women as sacrificial lamb among others.

Domestic Violence in Okoh's *In Our Own Voices*

Okoh's *In Our Own Voices* is an eye opener against the high level of domestic violence endured by women in Nigeria. In order to defend the position that the issue of domestic violence goes beyond cultures and ethnic boundaries in Nigeria, Okoh draws her characters from the various tribes that make up Nigeria. Even the use of the pronoun "our" in the title of the play suggests that the experience of domestic violence in Nigeria is not just against one woman but various women as can be found in the various societies in Nigeria. This is evident in the very first monologue of Woman 1 thus:

> ...domestic violence puts strain on our society as well as on our national economy for the violence occurs in varied forms in thousands of households across the nation. In the homes of the poor as well as of the rich. In the rural areas as well as

in the cities, women are suffering. Women are dying every day. Rivers of blood flows ceaselessly under the crushing weight of violence. And it is affecting all types of women (Okoh, 5)

Okoh's concern in the monologue above is to argue that domestic violence is no respecter of social or economic status but a wide fire set in motion by patriarchy to oppress and intimidate women. As Woman 1 laments her ordeal further, we come to terms with the reality that she is from a middle class family and a higher executive officer in the Nigerian Federal Civil Service who is financially sufficient but a survivor of domestic violence after several years of mental and physical abuse by her husband. The signs of domestic violence in Woman 1's marriage appeared quite early in her relationship but she was blindfolded by love and so could not protest it before she entered the marriage fully. According to her:

> The abuses really appeared after I've had my first child. He wanted to take full control of my life. I must account to him every movement I made and every action I took. But, playfully, playfully, I resisted then his possessive and controlling behaviours slowly manifested as the relationship grew. If I went for a visit without telling him, he got angry. Before giving me money for shopping, I must itemize what I wanted to buy and how much each item would cost. If per chance, I failed, due to price fluctuation, to buy everything I had listed, he would call me foul names: "Liar, cheat, the sly tortoise, wicked woman." Sometimes, to avoid his insult, I evaded demanding money from him, not even for his

> monthly contribution to the family upkeep. Even at that, he would still complain saying: 'you dunce, you idiot, you "yeye" woman!' You want to prove that you have money. That's why many men in this country don't want to marry educated women. You want your freedom and liberty. You want to compete with men. You want to be the head of the family. Okay, we shall see who is the head of this family. Alright, we shall see! You swine! (Okoh, 7)

Woman 1's bitter testimony above clearly locates her husband within the domain of patriarchal excesses as he tends to frown at Woman 1's enhanced educational status and sense of financial freedom. For him, his wife should be his slave that he can toss around at will rather than fitting into the shape of a help mate that the woman was naturally designed to be for man. It should be noted here that domestic violence does not only occur in physical abuse alone but includes mental torture of a partner by the other partner. Domestic violence is evident in the constant use of foul and abusive language on Woman 1 by her husband. Calling her by such derogatory names as "yeye woman' "dunce", "liar" and "sly tortoise" among others are clear evidences of mental abuse and consequently, domestic violence.

Woman 1 narrates the height of her experience of domestic violence by the hands of her husband in subsequent monologues where she portrays how the husband graduates from verbal abuse to physical abuse thus:

> One day, he returned home from work while I was still in the kitchen cooking his favourite dish: Pounded yam and *"genger"*

soup with bush meat. I quickly ran to the fridge to fetch him a glass of cold water. Casting a fleeting glance at the empty dining table, he stared at my face and growled: "Where is my food?" Before I could say anything, he landed a hot slap on my face, "Phiam!" The glass of water escaped my grip, shattered on the floor. The water spilled all over me. Why must I return from work to wait for you to cook? Answer "Phiam!" Have you been out frolicking with one of your bosses? Answer me! "Phiam!" He pushed me against the wall and gave me several punches. I slumped to evade the piercing punches. Then he kicked me and dragged me on the hard floor. In my stupor, I could hear the children crying and begging: "Daddy, please now, leave mummy alone! Daddy, please now, leave mummy alone! Daddy, you are hurting mummy. Please leave her alone!" He only left me alone, when he was tired of punching me… (Okoh, 8).

Woman 1's narrative above is a testimony of domestic violence through physical assault. It reveals how most men take advantage of their masculinity to brutalize their spouses over issues that would have been settled amicably through dialogue. As a matter of fact, one can hardly see any justification for Woman 1 husband's expression of anger except that he wants to demonstrate the usual patriarchal ego that men are superior to women. The latter is portrayed by the playwright as a failure both in the context of a husband and a father. Not even the presence of his children could restrain him from punching his wife. He obviously belongs to the class of Nigerian men who lumps their wives and children together as inferior beings especially girl-children.

Woman 1 also suffers sexual abuses by the hands of her husband. After receiving physical assault from her husband, it is expected that she would develop some form of emotional withdrawal from him but the husband thinks differently. He thinks that sexual submissiveness of his wife is part of her marital responsibilities regardless of her level of motivation or emotional arousal. For him, he has paid his wife's bride price and so his wife must submit to him sexually against all odds. This is another arrogant display of patriarchal excesses. Woman 1 puts it thus:

> Apart from the physical and psychological abuses, I was also a victim of sexual abuses. After receiving insults from him, I usually rebuffed his sexual advances. But without caring for my feeling or condition, he would assert: "You are my wife. I paid bride price on you. You belong to me. Whether you like it or not, I will have it. Come on, relax! Let's have a go! Don't push me. Don't push me. Humh! Humh!" He would lift up my nightgown to satisfy his desire, with me just lying on my back like a log of wood. When he was done and snoring, I would weep bitterly in silence. The fact that I was being used to satiate his sexual urges made me sick… (Okoh, 11).

The narrative put up by Woman 1 above captures the height of sexual molestation which most Nigerian women encounter in their marriages. The idea that a husband would see his lawfully wedded wife as a sex toy is highly disturbing and inhuman as it underscores the feminist protest that men consider themselves as superior species to women. From the narrative above, we also observe that the major motivation for her husband's show of unnecessary authority and superiority over Woman 1 is the fact that he paid her bride price. For most Nigerian men, bride price is the license to maltreat their spouses. Fondly, by paying the bride price, many men think they have already bought the women and so the woman becomes their commodity just like the upholstery in their rooms.

The pitiable state of Woman 1 is compounded by the fact that the Nigerian society does not provide the necessary checks and balances that would protect the fundamental human rights of women. Woman 1 runs to the police for protection against domestic violence meted on her by her husband but rather than offer her the protection she desires; the police prefer to treat the issue with trivial attention by distancing themselves in the case with the sentiment that "wife beating is a family affair." Through the disappointing sentiment launched by the police (a supposed law enforcement agency), Woman 1 is forced to the point of resigning to fate. To add salt to injury, her husband's family always do not see anything wrong in what their son, her husband does. Her mother-in-law (a fellow woman) prefers to threaten her further amidst her trauma rather than sympathize with her situation on hearing that she went to report to the police. Unfortunately, her mother-in-law who could not prevail on her son to stop battering his wife, stands out in defense of her son's domestic violence on his wife. She goes further to threaten Woman 1 thus:

> …Why are you involving the police in our family affair? Don't we have kindred and family-heads to arbitrate in dispute within our lineage? Educated woman! Are you no longer a Tiv woman? Where is your home training? Anyway,

> you are wasting your time. If the case ever makes it to court, it will remain there stagnant. Bet me! … (Okoh, 13).

It is the consistent battering she receives by the hands of her husband coupled with the cultural restrictions that forbids her to discuss her marital challenges outside her husband's lineage that compels Woman 1 to endure the consistent violence in her marriage to the point that she gets deformed by her husband through the pouring of acid on her body. Her husband's reason for pouring her acid is to deform her so that no other man would find her attractive anymore. The narrative of Woman 1 is not just pathetic but highly provoking as it bothers largely on lawlessness and outright disregard of the women's human rights in a country that is a signatory to various human rights charters including the *Universal Declaration of Human Rights*.

The case of Woman 11 is synonymous with that of Woman 1. However, Woman 11's experience bother on the inhuman treatment meted on women in Nigeria by conceiving them as mere commodities to be bought by men for a price. The narration from Woman 11 clearly locates her as a native of the eastern part of Nigeria. She is a victim of her own artistry as a dancer. As a way of community service, she was part of the cultural troupe stationed to dance at the village scare as a way of receiving an august visitor to her community. After a commendable performance as the lead dancer in the community dance troupe, Woman 11 is lumped up alongside other items to be presented as reception gift to the August visitor who happens to be the President of the country. Woman II narrates her case:

...Everybody rose up and applauded and praised me for having danced so well. Later, they called me aside and dressed me up with beautiful loom woven traditional material...Raising the microphone to his mouth once more the MC announced: "Mr. President, once more, we thank you for your visit to our state. Sir, according to our tradition, we hereby present to you some souvenirs: the best harvest from our farm, the best domestic foul from our poultry, the best bush meat from our forest, the best dried fish from our river, the best fabric material from our loom and because you are a very special guest, we added the best maiden dancer in our state... (Okoh, 22).

The narration above portrays the level of inhuman treatment and debasement meted on the women for no reason except that they belong to the female sex. The reward Woman 11 gets for volunteering to be part of community service and for being good at what she does is to be lumped up as a gift item for an August visitor whom she has never come in contact with. Without seeking her consent, Woman 11's community whisk her with other items like a commodity for her special visitor. In order to justify the fact that the conspiracy against women is largely societal, the August visitor (Mr. President) readily accepts Woman 11 the same way he accepts the other gift items. First, he rises up, smiles at Woman 11 broadly and then declares "all the gifts are accepted. Thank you!" (Okoh, 23). The President's patriarchal ego is evident in his acceptance of Woman 11 as one of the gift items offered him by the community. It therefore becomes scary to note that the President of the country who should lead by example in the protection of the women's human rights is the very person abusing such rights right in public. The same stretch of domestic violence is noted in the narrative of Woman III where she laments her pitiable condition as a victim of teenage pregnancy. At eleven Woman III was forcefully married off to Alhaji Musa- a man old enough to be her grandfather. The reason for the forced marriage was to enable her serve as her father's collateral for the debt owed to Alhaji Musa. First, she was tricked into moving into Alhaji Musa's house as a house help for Musa's wife who is heavily pregnant but there in the house, Alhaji Musa takes advantage of her innocence and begins to abuse her sexually. Woman III gets pregnant in the process and then the real complication sets in. Woman III narrates:

> One day, I was having unusual pains in my stomach. I informed my co-wife, and she went to fetch the birth attendant. The old woman spread a mat on the floor and asked me to lie down on it. She felt my stomach and said my uterus was contracting normally. Hopefully, very soon, the baby would come out. She rubbed some herbs on my stomach and on my waist. She opened my legs, looked into vagina and murmured: "It seems there is something preventing the baby from descending, despite strong uterine contractions. But don't panic," she said, "these things do happen quite often. It will come down. Let's wait." We waited. The baby did not come out. She did all she could to make the baby descend. Instead, the baby was playing pranks on us. It was changing its position every now and then. At one time, the lady said she saw what looked like the baby's

brow. At another time, it was what looked like the baby's buttock, and another time, it was what looked like the shoulder or knee. She was not sure. But the position of the baby was certainly abnormal. She then said we should pray to Allah for the baby to correct its position by itself… (Okoh, 29)

The scenario above clearly portrays the level of torture and violence which women in the remote part of Northern Nigeria undergo. First, a teenager at eleven is already betrothed to an old man in her grandfather's age bracket. The old man shamelessly goes ahead to abuse her sexually to the point of impregnating her without considering any biological rebound. Even in her pregnant state, she lacks the basic health care that would guarantee safe delivery. The old man responsible for the pregnancy cares less about the state of the health of the little girl he has forced into his household as a wife. Woman III is therefore left with the only option of being delivered by an inexperienced native birth attendant. Expectedly, the delivery process gets complicated and so emergency sets in but nothing tangible is done to save the mother and the child. The need to rush to the community health centre is quickly suggested by her co-wife but nothing still could be done at the moment because the old man (the man of the house) is not on ground to approve the decision. Woman III captures the moment thus:

> After some time, my co-wife suggested they should take me to the Health Center in the next community. The old lady replied, "Mama Halima, you want to put me in trouble? You know very well that in this our community A woman cannot

take such decision. That's the man's duty. Besides, women's movements are strictly under male control. None of us is qualified to take her to the hospital. We are women! So, we need a man to take her there, either your husband or a male surrogate." "But our husband is not at home. And there is no other man in this house except children", explained my co-wife. "We'll wait for your husband to return", said the old lady. "He left home at dawn, he may not return till dusk." "We'll wait for him patiently. Sit down. *Bari mu jira.*" "Look at how she is rolling from side to side on the mat. She has been in pain for many hours. We cannot allow her to continue to suffer like this. Already she looks emotionally drained. Please, do something", pleaded my co-wife. "But we cannot do anything in this circumstance. I repeat, we are women", said the old lady. "You are a well-respected woman in this community. You can explain to them why we had to disregard tradition", Suggested Mama Halima. "Babu! Not me-oh! As an elder, it is my duty to preserve the cultural traditions of our land. So, I say let's wait." "For how long are we going to wait?" "As long as it takes your husband to return." (Okoh, 30)

The accumulated delay in the labour process due to some unguarded and irrational patriarchal traditions complicates Woman III's pregnancy to the dangerous extent of losing the baby while also contracting the dreaded Vagina Vesico Fistula (VVF) as her pelvic is not mature enough to host pregnancy. The complications of VVF also includes the offensive smell from the vagina as a result of some rot and decay. In her state, she meets all kinds of stigmatization and abandonment even by the very man that put her in that condition.

Another manifestation of domestic violence against women is in the guise of circumcision. Woman IV who goes by the name, Obehi, suffers series of humiliation by the hands of husband because she could not conceive as a result of the complications gathered from a circumcision exercise she was subjected to in her teenage days by her parents. At first, Woman IV enters into a beautiful and lovely union with her husband but seven years into the marriage, her husband's family begin to agitate over her barrenness and in the process they compel their son, to pick another wife. Her husband settles for another wife who also bears him a son and from this development, Woman IV becomes a second class citizen in the marriage. First, she is asked out of her matrimonial room for the new wife to occupy and then given a smaller room. This very act points to the fact that she has lost her position as the first and senior wife of the family. Second, the husband resorts to assaulting her over the allegation that she intends to kill the new born son.

Again, Obehi is subjected to series of violence by her parents and husband respectively. In her teenage, her parents forced her to go through the pains and torture of female circumcision which leads to a major damage in her reproductive organ consequently, she is unable to conceive. Later, she goes into marriage and her barren condition opens another room for her husband to mete violence on her. In her frustration, she decides to walk out of the marriage in search of a new identity and new motivation to still exist as a human being with full potentials. Again her decision is obstructed by her cultural background which makes it impossible for a married woman to return to her father's house. One observes here that oppressive patriarchal values remain one of the greatest obstacles to women's freedom in Nigeria. A woman is abused in her marriage and yet does not have the right as a human person to walk out of such marriage even when the same system cannot protect her from the abuse. Woman IV's story is apparently a pathetic one even as those responsible for her condition go scot free.

The story of Woman V seems to be even deeper and graver than all the already viewed. Woman V is a product of the Ibo background where women are commonly held accountable for the death of their husbands regardless of the circumstances surrounding the death. Not minding that she is bereaved and so needs heart-warming consolation, the kinsmen of Woman V's deceased husband subject her to series of inhuman treatments all in the name of widowhood practice. Upon receiving the news of the demise of their son, the family of Woman V's husband summon her to the family compound in the community and then compel her to undergo series of oaths in order to prove her innocence in her husband's death. Not even the explanation from Woman V that her husband died of ghastly motor accident could convince her late husband's kinsmen that she has no hand in her husband's death. Woman V's narrative say it all:

> …They claimed they were not satisfied with my explanations that it is strange for a healthy man to die on his way to work. So, I should confess what I did to him before he left the house. I explained that I had nothing to confess. He left the house hale and sound. I was at work when I got a phone call

inviting me to come and identify his corpse. I knew about the circumstances of his death through police reports, based on eyewitness information. They insisted that I must take an oath to prove my innocence. They led me to the room where they laid his corpse on a bier, they scrubbed his body, squeezed the water into a bowl and gave it to me to drink, saying that if I die during the one year mourning period, that would confirm me guilty of his murder, which is an abomination. Therefore, my corpse would be thrown into the evil forest for vultures and wild animal to devour… (Okoh, 48)

More painful in the entire inhuman treatment meted on Woman V is the fact that the late husband's family do not consider the trauma which a woman undergoes in the loss of her breadwinner. They deliberately refuse to acknowledge the fact that every ideal marriage is anchored on love and so it is always a traumatic experience for any spouse to cope each time he or she loses a partner. The well-being of their daughter-in-law or sister-in-law means nothing compared to the death of their son and brother. It is also more painful to note that in the same culture the same dose of torture is never meted on the man who loses his wife. It becomes clearer that the Ibo culture on widowhood practice is one of the manifestations of violence unleashed on the woman just to subjugate her into acceptance that she is the inferior of the men folk. In the same Ibo culture, torturing the woman does not only end in accusing her of being responsible for her husband's death but goes to the extent of compelling her to mourn her husband in the most miserable of ways:

Soon after putting my husband in the grave, I was put into widowhood. The Umuada, daughters of the clan led me to an open compound, without any privacy. Surrounded only by the Umuada, I was stripped naked. After sacrificing a fowl, uttering some incantations to the ancestors they shaved the hairs on my head, my armpit and my pubic. Then, one of the old widows in the family bathed me, as a mark of final separation from my husband…From there, I was led to my place of seclusion, a dingy room without furniture, but with just an old mat placed on the hard floor, on which I was to sit and sleep throughout the wailing period…I was not allowed to go to anywhere during the first 40 days of confinement. Neither was I allowed to touch with my hands or any object nor any part of my body. For at this period, I was regarded to be unclean… (Okoh, 49).

It is interesting to note that the Umuadas who execute the humiliating treatment on Woman V in the guise of widowhood practice are her fellow women. One begins to wonder if the same-sex feelings does not run in their veins. The deep involvement of the Umuadas in the humiliation of their fellow women clearly demonstrates the fact that the maltreatment and oppression of women in most African societies draw motivation from patriarchal traditions that reduce women to mere commodities and properties acquired by men. Woman V's crime was nothing except that she lost her husband. Apart from the torture from the Umuadas, she also loses all her household properties that she acquired side by side with her husband to the husband's family because she refuses to be inherited by one of her deceased husband's siblings.

Okoh also portrays rape as a form of domestic violence meted on women in Nigeria. Through the character of Woman VI (known also as Tolu), a keen onlooker is exposed to the physical and mental torture associated with rape. As a child, Woman VI experiences rape through the hands of her own uncle who came squatting with her family in the city. As a result of the tight schedule of her parents, Woman VI, at a tender age, finds herself in the custody of Uncle Femi who rapes her and goes ahead to threaten that he would kill her if she reveals her rape experience to anyone. Out of fear, Tolu decides to conceal her traumatic experience and in the process she becomes used to her sensual experience with Uncle Femi. Tolu's real challenge begins from the very day that Uncle Femi was asked to leave the house for committing incest. According to Tolu:

> They discussed with Femi. And he moved out of our house. But that didn't deter us. It brought us closer together. Femi was coming to meet me at school. We would look for a quiet spot in the bush to have fun. Ha-ha-ha-ha! As time went by, I could never take my mind off Femi. If I didn't see him for a week, I was in a feat of anxiety. I would bite my finger or pull on my hair. Sometimes, I would tear my books or my clothes. Moreover, I began to have learning problems. My teachers complained to my parents. They were concerned, they advised me. But that didn't change anything. Ha-ha-ha-ha (Okoh, 61).

What began as parental negligence has grown into full psychological imbalance and moral decay on the part of Woman VI. Uncle Femi takes advantage of the consistent absence of her parents and abuses her sexually in the guise of looking after her, now Tolu has gotten used to constant sex and can no longer take her mind off it. Not even the exit of Femi could drop her appetite for sex. Tolu makes bold to confess thus:

> …But when Femi moved out of town, in his absence, I transferred my sexual desire to other men: classmates, teachers, pastors, gatemen! Whosoever was available at the moment of my burning desire became my target I lured them with my body language. You know what I mean. Ha-ha-ha-ha (Okoh, 67).

Tolu's uncontrollable appetite for sex was triggered by the early childhood sexual abuse she experienced through the hands of Uncle Femi. This was made possible as a result of negligence on the part of her parents in her upbringing as a child. Ironically, while she goes about her flirtatious lifestyle even as an adult of 35 years, the man responsible for her shattered sexual life is let go and establish and consequently run a decent family with a responsible woman as wife. Be that as it may, it suffices that so much blame is heaped on the society for making the constant mistake of exonerating the perpetrators of violence against women.

    A general examination of all the characters in this play clearly shows that Nigerian women are indeed victims of different shades of domestic violence. The violence meted on Nigerian women cut across religious, cultural, geographical and social boundaries. The perpetrators of these violence are both men and women of the respective societies in Nigeria. Okoh's *In Our Voices* is therefore a reflection of the contempt Nigerian women are made to endure. In an agreeable endnote, it suffices to say that women are treated as second class citizens in their own land for reasons that can hardly be explained beyond religious and cultural extremes. Apart from representing the various majority ethnicities in Nigeria, the playwright has portrayed the various trivial circumstances that ignite domestic violence on Nigerian women.

Conclusion/Way Forward

The study has made an attempt at examining the issue of domestic violence in Nigeria through the lenses of Julie Okoh's *In Our Own Voices*. In course of the study, it is observed that most women across the cultures and religions in Nigeria suffer one form of domestic violence or the other. What Okoh has inch-perfectly done is to chronicle the different shades of inhuman treatment meted on women in Nigeria in the name of respect for patriarchal traditions. Interestingly, this paper has made some findings that are worthy of mention. One of the major findings is sensed in the fact that patriarchy is one of the major reasons most Nigerian women suffer domestic violence in Nigeria. As evident in the play, most women are subjected to one form of violence or the other by either their father or husband as they are many times conceived as mere commodities that can be easily bought via bride price. Some of the women are willed away to a man as a collateral since their fathers could no longer service the debt owed. In the process, their prospective masters treat them with discontent, discord and mischief since they owe nobody any explanation.

This paper also attributes the rise in the cases of domestic violence in Nigeria to the weak and corrupt judicial system in the country. As a matter of fact, it is on course to say that it is habitually difficult for perpetrators of domestic violence against women to be prosecuted. A thorough reading of Okoh's *In Our Own Voices* reveals that none of the perpetrators of domestic violence was made to face the full wrath of the law. It is this weak judicial system in Nigeria that empowers most men to consistently perpetrate violence against women. The study also notes that the oppression, subjugation and maltreatment of women, which has a long history, is still in vogue in this 21st century amidst the spirit of globalization. Ironically, Nigeria is a signatory to most human rights charters and documents, yet it is a great encourager of the different shades of women's human rights abuse. As evident in the play, the bane of the matter exists in the fact that most of the laws of the land seem to work against women's expression of their fundamental human rights. Even the few women that dared to express such rights were greeted with outright rebuff and consequently violence whereas, they have no one to run to. The deduction here is that there are no proactive measures in the implementation of laws that protect the rights of women.

Way Forward
This paper sanctions the need for the law enforcement agencies and the judiciary in Nigeria to step up their games in ensuring that perpetrators of the abuse of women's human rights are brought to book without fear nor favour. Efforts should be made to penetrate most rural communities in Nigeria and charge them to court for endorsing cultural practices that endanger the mental and physical

health of Nigerian women. This is because a handful of these ferocious cultural practices are domiciled in the rural communities. Thus, it is recommended that the government enforce existing laws and consequently ensure the prosecution of offenders so as to serve as deterrent to others.

In another interest, women are also encouraged to speak up and speak out on matters that bother on the infringement of their fundamental human rights. The foregoing textual analysis has revealed that most of the women had their abuses when they were still infants and teenagers but due to certain reasons keep it within them for a greater part of their lives only to open up when they are no longer able to cope with the complications therein. Nigerian women must shout, they must speak and they must consciously spread the bitter truth about their abuses. They must shun the distraction of stigmatization and open up if the required change should come.

Culture is dynamic and not static. By this instance, there is the need for the traditional institution(s) in Nigeria to consciously review the diverse cultures in order to accommodate women as integral part of the society bearing freely the rights to self-expression. The torture which women are subjected to in some part of Nigeria in the guise of widowhood practices must be erased from such cultures. Cultures in Nigeria must also be reviewed in such a way that they should accommodate women's freedom and right (especially on matters relating to choice of married partners) without parental, family or societal interference.

Works Cited

Balogun, Abiodun. "Gender Crisis in Yoruba Thought: An Aftermath of Western Experience.
Journal of Cultural Studies; 97-106. 1999. Print

Childinfo. "Attitudes Towards Wife Beating". Childinfo.org. Retrieved September 8, 2013.

CNN Wire Staff. "Court in UAE Says Beating Wife, Child OK If no Marks are Left. Retrieved
January 24, 2014.

Csapo Gerald and Slater, Rodes. *Hypokrisis*. Penguin, 1994. Print

Encyclopedia Britannica. "The Causes and Effects of Domestic Violence." *Encyclopedia
Brtitannica* Inc. Retrieved October 12, 2017.

Fawole, Abiodun and Fawole, Abike. "Intimate Partner Abuse: Wife Beating Among Civil
Servants in Ibadan, Nigeria." *African Journal of Reproductive Health*. 9 (2),62, 2005. Print

Felson, Richard. *Violence and Gender Reexamined*. American Psychological Association.
Abstract, 2002. Print

Macmillan, Richard and Gartner, Rogers. "When She Brings Home the Bacon: Labor Force

Participation and The Risk of Spousal Violence Against Women." *Journal of Marriage and Family*.61, (4); 947-958. 1986. Print

Obi, Sylvester & Christopher Ozumba. "Factors Associated with Domestic Violence in South Eastern Nigeria". *Journal of Obstetrics and Gynaecology*, 27, (1), 2007, 75-78.

Odujirin, Ola. "Wife Battering in Nigeria." *International Journal of Gynaecology and Obsterics*. 41.(2), 1993. Print

Okemgbo, Christian and Odimegwu, Chinedu. Prevalence, Patterns and Correlates of Domestic Violence in Selected Igbo Communities of Imo State, Nigeria. *African Journal of Reproductive Health*.6, 2010, 101-114.

Okoh, Julie. *Mask*. Port Harcourt: Totan Publishers, 1988.

……*Towards Feminist Theatre*. Port Harcourt: University of Port Harcourt Press, 2012.

……*In Our Own Voices*. Pearl Publishers, 2021. Print

Oladepo, Temi, Yusuf, Ola and Arulogun, Suberu." Factors Influencing Gender Based Violence Among Men and Women in Selected States. *African Journal of Reproductive Health*.15, (4), 2011. Print

Oluremi, Fareo, Dorcas. "Domestic Violence Against Women in Nigeria". *European Journal of Psychological Research*. Vol.2, No.1; 212-222. 2015. Print

United Nations Office on Drugs and Crime. Strategies for Confronting Domestic Violence: A Resource Manual. New York, 2016. Print

Wilson, Edwin and Goldfarb, Alvin. *Theater: The Lively Art*. McGrawHill, 1999. Print

Wollstonecraft, Mary. *A Vindication of the Rights of Women*. New York: Prometheus Books, 1989.

World Health Organization. Gender, Equity, Human Rights: Gender BasedViolence. Geneva, WHO, 2015.

Cultural Influence on Gender Inequality In Osedebamen Oamen's *The Women Of Orena Are Wiser Than The Gods*

AMIRIHEOBU Frank Ifeanyichukwu, NWARU Chris and CHIMEZIEM Gloria Ernest-Samuel

Abstract

Till present, gender inequality, mostly against the female sex by their male counterparts, has ironically positioned as a serious menace plaguing the Nigerian state, thereby affecting the development in the society. This menace, masterminded traditionally by indigenous culture is visible when the socio-political cum economical fronts of the nation is being massively controlled by the men, while the women are left with little or nothing as portrayed in Osedebamen Oamen's *The Women of Orena Are Wiser Than The Gods*. Due to the ineffectiveness of the men towards managing the economic cum political strata of the Nigerian state as a result of corruption, the country is today besieged with issues which have affected its fronts politically, economically, socially, and religiously. These issues, resulting to unemployment, poverty, hunger, and suffering, thus increase death rate, sickness, and pain of the people, as well as underdevelopment to the state. Among the major findings is the contribution of culture as a major factor promoting gender inequality in Nigerian society, of which, it has provided impetus for creative punches in dramatic and theatrical representations by notable playwrights. Hence, by the adoption of Gender Schema Theory and Critical Discourse Analytical Approach, this study aims at investigating Osedebamen Oamen attempt to establish the effect of culture and gender inequality on the Nigerian state using the instrumentality of drama. The effect will create positive attitudinal change amongst Nigerians, thereby effectuating change around societies. The study recommends that the tradition and culture of the people should be checked to accommodate equality amongst the male and female genders.

Keywords: Conceptual, Discourse, Culture, Gender, Inequality.

Background to the study

From time immemorial, gender inequality, caused by unguided culture, has been positioned as a major menace in Nigerian society. Also considered a pervasive form of inequality around the world, it has been regarded as a pressing human right concern. Inequality amongst women and men, boys and girls, play out across all area of life in every country, cutting across both public institutions – governance, private spheres, families, and households. Gender inequality is reflected in the daily realities of women and girls' lives. While considering the dimensions of economic gender inequality, women who make less than men in the formal work sector more likely live in poverty, are less likely to participate in the formal work sector, and also do a larger share work in the household sector (Rewhorn, 2020, 68). The dimensions of political gender inequality, according to (Kleven & Landais, 2017, 132), include women's lower representation in elected office and lower representation in political and corporate appointments.

On the political base, women according to Mary (2021, 15) are given 35% right while the men have 65%. This percentile is visible as Nigeria is yet to produce female presidents, governor, senate president and other highly reputable positions in governance. In the family, wives are not given equal attribute with the husband due to the fact that the girl child is taught on how to be submissive to her husband right from childhood (15). In the opinion of Fantom and Serajuddin (2016, 267), women are not allowed to handle high positions. Instead, they are allowed the positions of deaconess, women leader, and other lower positions strategically placed under their male counterparts.

Culturally, women are not allowed to perform some sacred acts unless they are ordained by the deity who automatically make them equal to men. Consistently, men were trained not to partake in most domestic chores such as cooking, sweeping, fetching of water and firewood, which are exclusively shifted aside to women. In favour of this position, Kilmer & Rodriguez (2017, 37) averred that women were relegated to the domestic facilities that were not renovated or valued. In line with this, Adegbite and Machethe (2020, 56) observe that the implementation of gender differences are created and sustained by society through its traditional customs, conventions, norms and regulations.

Actually, the tradition or cultural beliefs in Nigeria as a typical patriarchal society see women as properties to her husbands who have the moral right to decide the actions which the woman must take - whether she will come out to join the active politics is a matter which the man will decide since the tradition has inscribed her will to the man (Aina, 2012, 45). In the concept of inequality against the female gender, there is no relationship between the male and female, owing to the fact that women are like slaves working to enrich their husbands and masters, who the tradition has ascribed the pillar of the family and the key to continuation and retention of the family name (CEIC, 2019, 754).

The effects of gender inequality in Nigeria has instead metamorphosed or diffused, overtime, exerting a pervasive, albeit, negative influences on all facets of the Nigerian society – economic, political, social, religious, etc. These influences include abuses of power through corrupt practices. The effect is seen on the increase in poverty rate, pervasive hardship, suffering, pain, death, and sicknesses accrued on the populace (Isiksal & Chimezie, 2016, 56). It has also bought underdevelopment, devaluation of currency, and bad identity to the nation at large. This has also increased the issues of terrorism, manifested in acts such as kidnapping, youth restiveness, incessant killings, suicide bombing, armed robbery, prostitution, drug abuse, illegal oil bunkering, and other malicious acts (Amaka, 2020, 76).

This issue has generated series of discourse within the Nigerian socio-political strata and has provided impetus for creative portraiture in dramatic and theatrical representations by notable playwrights. Thus, the nature and effects of the menace as explained in Osedebamen Oamen's *The Women of Items are Wiser than the gods* are the main thrust of the study. The play specifically interrogate how tradition, norms, value system and occupation of the Nigerian people help in promoting the issue of gender inequality, thus, revealing that culture is basically made to satisfy the people and not to enslave few and favouring the other.

Aim and Objectives of the Study
The aim of this study is to critically analyze the issue of culture and gender inequality in the Nigerian society as portrayed in Osedebamen Oamen's *Women of Orena are wiser than the gods*.
The specific objectives of the study includes the following:

1. To find out the depth of critical discourse generated from the portraiture of culture and gender inequality in Osedebamen Oamen's *Women of Orena are wiser than the gods.*
2. To examine the context of the portrayal of culture and gender inequality in Osedebamen Oamen's *Women of Orena are wiser than the gods.*
3. To advance solutions to the issues of culture and gender inequality as portrayed in Osedebamen Oamen's *Women of Orena are wiser than the gods.*

Research Questions

The following research questions will be considered as guide to this study.

1. In what ways does Osadebamen's Women of Orena portray culture and gender inequality?
2. What is the basic context of culture and gender inequality depth of critical discourse generated from the portrayal of culture and gender inequality in Osedebamen Oamen's *Women of Orena are wiser than the gods?*
3. What are the solutions to the issues of culture and gender inequality in Osedebamen Oamen's *Women of Orena are wiser than the gods?*

Scope of the Study

The focus of this study is primarily on culture and gender inequality as portrayed in selected Nigerian dramas. The selected play for discourse is Osedebamen Oamen's *The Women of Items are wiser than the gods.*

Gender Redefined

On a more clearer note, the concept 'Gender' according to Obafemi (2016, 265) was used for the first time in the 1940s by John Money in a discourse meant to legitimize sex change, and it began to be employed in the social sciences from the late 1960s onwards, hence from that period the question of gender has come to be central to discussions of social life (Turner, 2006 in Rewhorn, 2020, 167). However the real emergence of gender as a concept on its own is largely associated with the second-wave feminism which drew attention to sexual divisions in society and to the patterns of social difference and inequality that arose. All these conditions according to Rewhorn (2020, 452) need to be fulfilled so as to reach mutual understanding.

Besides, poets, playwrights, and most of the time authors create their own world of imagination that they believe into to reflect what they think are going on in the world they populate. To achieve this, it is a necessity to incorporate sociolinguistics in their productions. Rewhorn pragmatic and sociolinguistic investigation of the play is critical of the underlined themes of the play – cultural conflicts, generational conflicts and ideological differences between the new and the old.

Concept of Inequality

On the one hand, inequality as a concept is the state of not being equal, especially in statues, rights, and opportunities. It is a concept very much at the heart of social justice theories (Amaka, 2020, 231). However, Yunusa (2019, 213) avers that it is prone to confusion in public debate as it tends to mean different things to different people. Some distinctions are common though. For instance, many authors and critics distinguish "economic inequality," mostly meaning "income inequality," "monetary inequality," or, more broadly, inequality in "living conditions," (Klevan &Landais, 2017, 635).

Others further distinguish a right-based, legalistic approach to inequality-inequality of rights and associated obligations, for instance, when people are not equal before the law, or when people have unequal political power (IMF, 2020, 234). At its most basic, it refers to the hierarchical distribution of social, political, economic, and cultural resources (Abendroth et al, 2017, 245). A closely related concept according to Isiksal & Chimezie (2016, 241) is that of stratification, a more specific and technical term that refers to a model of social inequality that specifies the relationship between particular variables, such as wealth and social standing.

Nature of Gender Inequality
Lucidly, gender inequality is discrimination on the basis of sex or gender causing one sex or gender to be routinely privileged or prioritized over another. Gender equality is a fundamental human right and that right is violated by gender based discrimination. Gender disparity starts in childhood and is right now limiting the lifelong potential of children around the world – disproportionately affecting girls (Fantom & Serajuddin, 2016, 312).

Gender inequality differs from types of inequality in significant ways, so we cannot tacitly assume that gender inequalities will trace the same path as other inequalities. Gender inequality exist when men (or women) enjoy a disproportionately larger share of some valued well positions such as political power, economic or religious positions (Mary, 2021, 27). In furtherance to this opinion, Alubo (2012, 123) earlier noted that 'men and women can differ in any number of domains, so gender inequality intersects other types such and education, economic, political, and so on'. To this, Mary (2021, 27) writes that women may be gaining on men in some domains and falling further behind in other domains.

Even so, Aina and Olayode (2012, 98) noted that in a few domains, such as life expectancy, women have the advantage, so declining gender inequality in this instance refers to man gaining on women. These features of gender inequality according to Quentin (2017, 28) imply that it is important to examine the domains of gender inequality separately. In short, with respect to political power and economic activities, the disparities between women and men in Nigeria are sizeable (Lori, 2013, 90).

On a more serious note, Nigerian playwrights, like their counterparts across the globe, according to Sultana (2016, 98) have subscribed to the mimetic and reflective functions of literature through the subject matter and themes of their plays. One of the critical issues that have occupied the centre stage of dramatic criticism in Nigeria and other parts of Africa is the representation of gender in male and female authored texts (Egya, 2014, 86).

More so, Soyinka, in his *The Lion and the Jewel*, consciously or unconsciously has represented male characters as strong, powerful and metaphorically as a lion, a symbol of irresistible power. They are also portrayed as initiator, doer of something, and commander in chief, the king while their female counterparts (Sidi, Sadikou) are represented as goals and/or beneficiaries of men's actions and associated with processes of sensing and of emotion (Patrice &Albert, 2015, 423). To expatiate further, in *The Trials of Brother Jero* and *The Lion and the Jewel*, Soyinka's representation of women is consistent with the overall Yoruba gender ideologies of male 'perfection' and female 'imperfection'.

In like manner, Chinua Achebe's novel *Things fall Apart*, ex-rays the Igbo individuals' patriarchal pop culture which needs a strict framework about behavioral traditions as stated by sexual orientation. These traditions determinedly confine the opportunity about Igbo ladies also help will fortify era following the idea that Igbo men are better than the Igbo women. In the novel, ladies of the Igbo tribe are unpleasantly mistreated, thus are powerless; they are deprived to dictates to their part in their society.

Extensively, *Things Fall Apart* is a standout amongst the novels, which exposes those parts for ladies. In this novel, Mascot, what's more ladylike social character and dialect examples reflect a uniquely negative social mentality towards womanliness and an acquaintanceship of ladies is also shortcoming. This novel may be additionally an affirmation of the social attitudes towards sex, by stressing the shortcoming of womanliness and the profits of Mascot self-destructive considerations and conduct those Igbo individuals underscore that sex stratification for their society, this furthermore guarantee the continuation for patriarchy.

On the contrary, Ola Rotimi's ideology on culture and gender inequality, mostly in his play *Our Husband Has Gone Mad Again*, differs from that of Wole Soyinka and Chinua Achebe. For instance, Jegede, (2015, 254) states that the drama specifically satirizes the political corruption associated with the Nigerian society; the major object or subject of attack and derision in the play is Lejoka-Brown. He believes so much in his military intelligence in outsmarting everybody. The playwright lampoons his protagonist's idea about politics with military intelligence and sagacity. That is why Lejoka-Brown insists that politics is a source of wealth-making. In the play, politics is seen as a profession where one loots public fund, a social transformer and image raiser for whosoever is involved in it at the expense of the masses and national security.

Finally, on the ideology of female interpretation on feminism and culture, Canice and Nicholas (2015, 132) aver that "Zulu Sofola was one of the foremost African female writers whose feminist crusade stand opposed to separatist, radical and revolutionary feminism produced by the whirlwind of feminism blowing across the globe because of their aspiration towards achieving same sex status with men, shunning marriage, etc". Therefore, the preoccupation in this research is to assess the impact of Sofola's juxtaposition of the conservative and the radical feminist ideological conceptions within the African feminist agenda. This paradox of liberalism and radicalism in *The Sweet Trap* provides a suitable case study for this paper as well as for exploring Sofola's impact on other Nigerian feminist writers (Canice & Nicholas, 2015, 53).

African feminist theories according to Obadiegwu (2009, 213) emerged from this feminist movements that project both liberal and radical/separatist feminisms. Feminism has predominantly altered perspectives of gender issues in Africa. Despite ideological dichotomy, African feminism should according to Ogundipe (2007, 251) stem from the theory of liberal feminism which projects feminism as"… a body of social philosophy that advocates and actively seeks the liberation and humanization of women in society". Hence, radical and separatist feminism which seeks to achieve same sex status with men are antipodal to African culture.

Zulu Sofola according to Udengwu (2009, 542) attempts the concretization of the liberal feminist theory in her play. Initially, she uses the juxtaposition dramatic technique to place the liberal and radical feminist groups side by side. Sofola uses resolution of the conflict of her play to make a strong statement on African Feminism. Nevertheless, The Sweet Trap relies on the duality of Sofola's plot, her dramatic technique that juxtaposes opposites to explore both radical and liberal feminism (Canice & Nicholas, 2015, 423).

Effects of Gender Inequality in Nigeria
This is a term referring to the understanding that when a society invests in girls the effects are deep for the girls, multiple for society and drives sustainable development. The consequence of prolonged marginalization of women is that most women tend to be emotionally dependent especially on men. As mentioned in Paulo Friere (1987, 32), Amaka (2020, 231) writes that such emotional dependency referred to as 'necrophilia behaviour,' the destruction of life – their own or that of the oppressed fellows". This explains why individual women and women organizations have continued to make social appeal to men to give them power and to carry them along in politics, economy, and in other social relationships (Lippa, 2015, 241).

Concept and Meaning of Culture
The origin of the Latin word cultura is clear. It is a derivative of the verb colo (infinitive colere), meaning "to tend," "to cultivate," and "to till," among other things (UNDP, 2019, 541). According to Archibong (2018, 47) it can take objects such as ager, hence

agricultura, whose literal meaning is "field tilling." Another possible object of the verb colo is animus ("character").The etymological analysis of "culture" is quite uncontroversial (Mary, 2020, 35). However, in the field of anthropology, the situation is much more complex. Definitions of culture abound and range from very complex to very simple. For example, a complex definition was proposed by Para-Mallam (2017, 24) that culture is "transmitted and created content and patterns of values, ideas, and other symbolically meaningful systems as factors in the shaping of human behavior". An even less easily comprehensible definition was provided by Worsdale &Wright (2020, 3), who averred that "by culture we mean an extra somatic, temporal continuum of things and events dependent upon.

From the foregoing, it is established that the nature of gender inequality in Nigeria which may be seen on the political, economic, social, and religious strata is alarming despite the interrogation and possible recommendations by scholars and dramatists. To this, lots of issues which range from poverty, hardship, suffering, and pain are affecting the people and regions of the country have remained underdeveloped. It is on this note that the study aims at identifying Osadebamen Oamen's position on the cause and solution of gender inequality in his play *Women of Orena are wiser than the gods*.

Gender Schema Theory
Gender Schema Theory, propounded in the year 1981 by Sandra Bern provides the mode by which this study is shaped. When encapsulated, Gender Schema Theory provides the way by which people learn a complex network of gender-related concepts and

symbols from their culture. The ultimate sources of gender schemas are cultures, families, teachers, and peers (Lippa, 2015:108).

Gender schema theory is a social-cognitive theory about how people in society become gendered from an early age and the impact of this gendering on their cognitive and categorical processing throughout the lifetime. Children develop ideas and theories about what it means to be masculine or feminine (called gender schemas) from an early age and use these theories to categorise information, make decisions, and regulate behavior. According to Bern (1981), gender-schematic people are more likely to divide their world and regulate their behavior based on gender, whereas for gender a schematic people, gender is a less important category and thus they are less likely to organise information or regulate their behavior based on gender.

Bern developed Gender Schema Theory in order to investigate and place greater focus on the ways in which society creates and enforces the categories of gender. Bern further explained gender schema theory as follows: Specifically, gender schema theory argues that because American culture is so gender polarizing in its discourse and its social institutions, children come to be gender schematic (or gender polarizing) themselves without even realising it. Gender schematicity, in turn, helps lead children to become conventionally sex-typed.

That is, in imposing a gender-based classification on reality, children evaluate different ways of behaving in terms of the cultural definitions of gender appropriateness and reject any way of behaving that does not match their sex. In contrast to Kohlberg's cognitive-developmental account of why children become sex-typed, this alternative account situates the source of the child's motivation for a match between sex and behavior, not in the mind of the child, but in the gender Polarisation of the culture (Bern 1993, pp. 125–126).

In her influential work (1983, 8), Sandra questioned why sex became the important organising principle around which children built their identities, rather than other readily available categories such as race, religion, or even eye color. Sandra called this the "why sex?" Question; why is it that sex becomes such an important difference in the lives of very young children. Sandra argued that there's a presumption that sex differences are naturally and inevitably (8) more important to children than other differences. Sandra explains that Gender Schema Theory contains two fundamental presuppositions about the process of individual gender formation. First, that there are gender lenses embedded in cultural discourse and social practice that are internalised by the developing child.

Second, that once these gender lenses have been internalised they predispose the child, and later the adult, to construct an identity that is consistent with them. This model of enculturation is sufficiently general to explain how all cultural lenses are transferred to the individual, not just gender lenses (Starr & Elieen, 2017, 23).

Gender Schema Theory, identifies or interrogates the nature of gender inequality as influenced by the tradition, norms, value system, occupation, and general way of life of the Nigerian society will help to critically guide this study. This is so because the study interrogates how Osedebamen Oemen portrays the issue of gender slavery, marginalisation, intimidation, discrimination, against the maidens who are used to reminisce the crime caused by King Omena the chief antagonist.

Finally, with this theory, the study will equally interrogate how the dead princesses where negatively brainwashed by their parents to be able to accept marrying the son of the antagonist, knowing that such marriage is a death trap.

Methodology

This research work employs the critical discourse analysis research approach of the qualitative research method. It involves explaining the issue, describing, analyzing and interpreting data on the basis of culture and gender discrimination in Nigeria as portrayed in Osedebamen Oamen's *Women of Orena are wiser than the gods*. It is qualitative because it deals with the analysis by a notable Nigerian playwright, and descriptive because it involves the use of ideas to describe and analyze the issue of culture and gender inequality within the play contexts. To achieve this, the study employs the primary and secondary sources. The primary source is the play text and the researchers' ideas concerning the issue of culture and gender inequality in Nigeria, while the secondary source includes materials from the institutional publications, articles, journals, text books, internets, research materials, amongst others.

Synopsis of *Women of Orena are wiser than the gods*.

The play presents the collective resistance by the women of Orena against the gods for undue revenge through armistice, cooperation and adherence to deliberate abstinence from child bearing. They took advantage of being the only endowed source of procreation and threatened to kill the existence of the gods in their consciousness.

The play revolves around Ataje the central character who painstakingly mobilized the women of Orena to evolt against the male due to the subsequent and painful deaths of six crown princesses, married to Prince Zolobo by the Chiefs and the retrieval of Omeme, the 7th crown princess who is supposed to put an end to the curse that was placed on the royal household due to the taboo created by King Omena and Queen Atohan, when Prince Zolobo as a child fell from the mothers back when beaten by King Omena. As part of Orena culture and tradition, seven princesses are to be sacrificed to appease the gods, which will in turn keep the royal lineage.

    The women, led by Ataje, questions the notion of sacrificing seven innocent maidens, thereafter, highlighting the bias nature of the gods, king, chiefs and the men in the community, who considers Orena women as nothing in the society. To change this level of inequality, the women decide to show their importance by blocking the means of procreation. With this, they believe that their worth will be well noticed by the men, who will in turn, respect their gender. This they did by deciding that they will never get pregnant or give birth to young ones for their husbands unless the gods and the king finds lasting solution to the killing of young maidens in the royal family.

    After five years, the women was called back to take back the decision and start bearing children that will in turn till farm lands for their husbands, but the women, led by Ataje refused. This obviously made King Omena and the chiefs to pacify Otua into believing that he can change the decision of the gods by yielding to the demands of the women.

The play comes to an end when the solution to the death of the princesses was discovered, women opinion in issues that concerns their life, right, and general obligations are put to consideration.

Women of Orena Are Wiser Than The Gods and theme of culture and gender inequality

From the foregoing, it is revealed that the tradition or cultural beliefs in Orena ably representing the Nigerian society as a typical patriarchal society that sees women as properties of their fathers and husbands who have the sole moral right to decide the actions taken by the women. In the concept of inequality and subordination of women to men, there is no relationship, and women are like slaves working to enrich their husbands, their masters, who the tradition ascribed the pillar of the family and the key for the continuation and retention of the family name, thus, family legacies are adequately protected. It is against this backdrop that the chiefs in the play decided to convince King Omena to persuade Prince Zolobo to prepare to welcome the new bride that will occupy the vacuum in his heart. Chief Otu's statement below justifies it:

> **Chief Otu:** My lord, you know our tradition does not permit you to grieve for more than one day. Again, our son cannot remain in the cold for more than a day. Let him make his choice tonight, by tomorrow evening, the vacuum is filled (19).

This ideology, such as in the Nigerian society is prevalent despite the pain, suffering and anguish that the women go through. In the play, the chiefs through the permission of King Omena, searches for more wives to bear an heir for prince Zolobo without considering that the young virgins are people's daughters and humans. Such as most men in the Nigerian society, the chiefs believe that women and girls of Orena are worthless; no serious attention should be given to them even at death. Evidence of this is seen in the play when Chief Omoni reminded King Omena that:

> **Chief Omoni:** …by our tradition, no man mourns his wife for more than seven days. My lord, we must begin our search for another belle that will match position of the crown princess (20).

In furtherance to this assertion, Chief Otu, while addressing King Omena too careless about the death of the first crown princess assert that:

> **Chief Otu:** My lord, you know our tradition does not permit you to grieve for more than one day. Again, our son cannot remain in the cold for more than a day. Let him make his choice tonight, by tomorrow evening, the vacuum is filled (19).

This is evidence in the Nigerian society where men that loses their wives quickly remarries while the women are meant to mourn their husbands for years and most are lured according to tradition to remarry her husband's brother or any of the husbands relatives.

On a more serious note, the issue of gender inequality has risen as a major issue in the Nigeria society that even the few privileged women that has attained political and economic positions in the

Nigerian society are subjected to the directives of their superiors who are most often men. This is also visible in the play when the highest position occupied in Orena community is the position of the queen, which Atohan and queen Oyeme occupied. Despite occupying this position as the first and second queens due to their marriage to the king, they were very submissive to King Omena, Prince Zolobo and the chiefs. The evidence of this is seen when queen Atohan was seen crying when Otua and Ogidan, the two seers in the community pointed that the gods revealed that she was the cause of the death of the dead princesses. Otahan's speech below justifies it:

> **Atohan:** (In tears) what evil will please me against my son? I married His Majesty so as to take care of him and bring forth kings that will take after him on this throne (62).

By this, she, as queen, knelt down before her husband King Omena and the chiefs and pleaded for mercy. While on the same note, it is against the culture of Orena people for the king or the prince to kneel before anyone or mistakenly fall on the floor with their front or their back. It is as a result of the fallen of Prince Zolobo at Queen Otahan's back that made the gods to lay a cause against the royal family in detriment of innocent maidens. To this, Ataje specifically questions the high rate of inequality and marginalisation against the women when she painstaking thwarted the decision of the gods for demanding for the sacrifice of seven virgin princess that must die as soon as they are married to Prince Zolobo. Ataje's speech when the Seer revealed the cause of the death of the princesses justifies this statement:

Ataje: Why is it that it is the innocent wife who bears the penalty? A man beats his wife with a child on her back. The man did not respect the innocent child and the Gods did nothing to the man, his wife or son but continues to kill every woman that is married to the child at adulthood. Why not the man, his wife or the child? Why the innocent wife? It is deceptive. I am going home with my daughter (101).

This singular issue in the play is equivalent in the Nigerian society where the women are not considered and are maltreated by their husbands and men in the society. To this, Ataje pleaded that her husband should join forces with the women to demonstrate against King Omena and the Chiefs. Her statement below justifies it: **Ataje:** Join us to put forces together against the forces that cut the lives of crown princesses shot in their prime (87).

When she discovered that Kali her husband has refused to form alliance with her against the King and the Chiefs, rather, he decided to give Omeme their daughter out for marriage to Prince Zolobo without Ataje's consent, Ataje decided to summon the women of Orena to revolt against the men. Her statement to the women below justifies it:

Ataje: My beloved women of Orena, is it a crime to be a woman? Six of our children have mysteriously been plucked by an unseen hand of death…the king and his chiefs have deliberately decided not to bother, not even to find out the cause. Could it be that they know the cause and they deliberately mean to sacrifice our children for an unknown cause? Do we marry them so as to give birth to crown princesses in their graves? Shall we continue to give out our daughters to the royal grave? They have taken another young woman again as a wife. We should expect another knock on the door of mother earth.

So the women, led by Ataje decided to revolt, demanding that cultural issue that has maliciously affected them through the untimely death of their maidens should be addressed.

It is also observed in the play such as in the Nigerian society that the culture permits the men to seek for another wife few days after their dead wives are laid to mother earth, while the woman is meant to mourn her bereaved husband for years. She will even wear mourning cloth in that period to indicate she is mourning her husband so that other men may not pass advances against them but the men are allowed to go about their daily life as if nothing happened. Atohan's statement below justifies it:

Ataje: …many who died were either openly or secretly married, yet they died with or without fourteen days of mourning. The King and his Chiefs are dancing upon the graves of our young ones. The king and his Chiefs are dancing upon the graves of our young ones. How pleasant is such a dance in our eyes? Shall we then continue to watch such a dance with aseptic innocence? (88).

Vividly, in the cultural and marriage institution choice of life partner, young girls are denied the right to choose their husbands, or even forced into early marriage, into the life of a man whether love is there or not. This is evidenced when in the play the chiefs decided to persuade the parents of the dead crown princesses to give them out to prince Zolobo even when they are aware that the princesses will end up like the others. More so, in marriage institution, some practice polygamy while some cases resulted to progeny syndrome; families without a male child are deprived some rights and privilege. This could be seen in the play when Kali decided to give out his only daughter as wife to Zolobo because he wanted to gain recognition and fame in the community, mostly as his family is deprived some rights and privileges in the community. Chief Ello's speech below justifies this statement:

Chief Ello: We desire your honour, so do you deserves ours. To achieve this, we want you to entrust your daughter in our care. It is an honour to be entrusted with the care for a human being considering human complexity (80).

Kali's statement further justifies this statement:

Kali: ...please allow them to take her to the palace. I expect you to be grateful to god that our child is worthy to marry the crown prince. Even if she dies, at least, we remain the king's in-laws (65).

Such as in the play, in some Nigerian societies, this enhances involvement in polygamous families and the concept of inequality and subordination of women to men. Furthermore, women are being restricted from access to sources of power both economically, politically, socially and otherwise.

Even at that, most Nigerian culture gives the male child the freedom of association but deprives the female child such freedom; such as, the male child is allowed to sexual knowledge at tender age, while the girl child is meant to keep herself sacred for her supposed husband. To keep to this standard, a white cloth is given to the husband to spread on the matrimonial bed before meeting with his newly married wife. If the white cloth is stained with blood, it means that the girl is pure, thus, brought honour to her husband and her family but if the white cloth is not stained, it then means that the new wife has been sleeping around with men in the community which is against the tradition of the Orena people. Evidence of this is seen in the play when King Omena corrected Queen Atohan when he said:

> **Queen Atohan:** …if my son did not meet her at home that means she brings a huge sum of shame upon her parents. It shows she is not properly cultured. But I trust my in-laws; they are expecting the immaculate white cloth stained with their daughter's blood (6).

This act, though not plausible in today's society, but serves as microcosm of cultural barriers which ultimately deprives the female child the equal right and privilege with the male child, mostly as it concerns her sexual life. King Omena, while stressing on the importance of girl child virginity to Prince Zolobo, noted that:

> **Prince Zolobo:** The joy you witnessed in your in-laws house signifies the importance of it. It shows that your wife is well cultured. She brought honour to her family. It indicates that

your wife is virtuous. Aren't you glad that you are the first man ever to pass through that route? (10).

Such as in the play where the female virginity is regarded as most sacred, thus, defines the level a cultured family, same is applied in the Nigerian society where any girl that is not a virgin is considered not pure and those that have no sex experience are considered pure. They do not consider the emotion and trauma the girl child who have been deprived due sex pass through on regular bases.

Conclusively, the playwright obviously advocated in the play that the emotion of the women of Orena, such as some women in the Nigerian state should be respected. On this note, the playwright insist that the only way to achieve this is to have a close look at the culture which is the sum total of the way of life of a certain people and address it in favour of the people. He plainly stated that the gods which constitute the culture only vents their anger on the women but acquits the men even with higher sin. Ataje's speech concludes it:

Ataje: henceforth, the gods must not hold any woman responsible for a backed male child that fell, or the future wife of the child, if it were a female child, would the gods have reacted the same way? (108).

This statement concludes the thematic thrust of the play which is targeted at how culture promotes gender inequality in the Nigerian society.

Conclusion

From the study, it is pertinent to deduce categorically that in the Nigerian society, culture is the chief cause why women remain pawn both in the hands of nature and the authority of their husband. When we talk of the culture of a people, our reference point is the totality of their way of life. It consists of all the ideas and principles guiding the individuals' life, individually and collectively which include arts, beliefs, customs, inventions, language, technology and traditions. Culture is very important in human development. Human culture represent among other things the historical accumulation of human values. The concept of culture as a dynamic phenomenon gives impetus to the search for progress in all social sectors and branches of learning, and even to the belief and constant refinement of cultural experience. This will further enhance the beauty of human nature together with its immediate environment; and often times affect the female gender on all fronts. In traditional Nigerian societies, a woman, as defined by culture, is subordinate to her husband. This culture of female subordination is not only limited to her husband but also to all the members of her husband's family. A woman derived her status from being a wife and a mother. She performs these two major roles by having as many children as possible; hence she enjoys a sense of fulfillment by giving birth to a male child (Obafemi, 2016, 231). This power imposed on the male gender against the female gender obviously indicates that women are not respected and their existence is primarily to satisfy the male and family ego. Such as in the play also, women in the Nigerian society are often humiliated, downtrodden and restricted in various ways which includes political, social and economic.

Recommendations

The study recommends that:
1. As observed in the play, culture is the chief cause of gender inequality in the Nigerian society, societal obstacles of religion, tradition and other obnoxious beliefs must be broken, women should not be domesticated, they have to enjoy right to work and associated benefits as men.
2. Women, such as in the play should strive more in the advocacy for gender equality by continuous involvement in political, social and economic fronts, targeted at improving the female gender that will in turn better the Nigerian society.
3. Considering the disparity in decision making which resulted to death of the crown princesses in the play, which is also prevalent in the Nigerian society in the recent time, it is therefore important that the act of governance should be diversified to capture the interest of women through adequate representation.

References

Amaka, Thank-God. Re-Socialization, Gender Equality, and Women Access to Justice in Nigeria. *International Journal of Advanced Research in Social Sciences, Environmental Studies and Technology*, 5(4), 2020: 60-74

Abendroth, Kennedy, Melzer Sunday, Kalev Amaka & Tomaskovic-Devey, Doris. (2017). Women at work: women's access to power and the gender earnings gap. *ILR Review*, 7(1), 2017: 190-222.

Adegbite, Onojie & Machethe, Clifford. Bridging the financial inclusion gender gap in smallholder agriculture in Nigeria: an untapped potential for sustainable development. *Journal of World Development*, 12(2), 2020: 104-755.

Archibong, Bennita. Historical origins of persistent inequality in Nigeria. *Oxford Development Studies*, 4(1), 2018: 325-347.

CEIC, "*Nigeria government debt percentage of GDP 1981–2019*", available at: https://www.ceicdata.com/en/indicator/nigeria/government-debt--of-nominal-gdp, accessed 25 September, 2022. 2019, Online

Fantom, Neuton, & Serajuddin, Umar. The World Bank's classification of countries by income. *Policy Research working paper*; no. WPS 7528, World Bank, Geneva. 2016. Print.

International Monetary Fund, "*World economic outlook database*", available at: Imf.org, (accessed December 24, 2021), 2020, online.

Isiksal, Aliya & Chimezie, Ojiego, Impact of industrialization in Nigeria. *European Scientific Journal*,12(1), 2016: 328-339.

Kilmer, Joyce & Rodríguez, Raymond, Ordinary least squares regression is indicated for studies of allometry. *Journal of Evolutionary Biology*, 30(3), 2017: 4-12.

Kleven, Hurt & Landais, Charles. Gender inequality and economic development: fertility, education and norms. *Nigerian Journal of Economic and Development*, 8(1), 2017: 180-209.

Lippa, Ray. *Gender, Nature, and Nurture*. London: Lawrence Erlbaum Associates, Inc. 2015. Print.

Mary, Onyebuchi.Gender and the imperative of women participation in governance: Prospects and challenges. *International Journal of Advanced in Social Sciences, Environmental Studies & Technology*, 6(2),2020: 323-334.

Obafemi, Olori. Gender, Politics and Theory. In Hassan A. S. et al (eds), *Democratic culture in Democracy and Development in Nigeria*, Lagos: Concept Publication Limited. 2016, print.

Osedebamen, Oamen. The Women of Orena are wiser than the gods. Ibadan: Evans Brothers Nigeria Publishers Limited. 2009, print.

Para-Mallam, Friday. Gender equality in Nigeria. *Gender Equality in a Global Perspective, ROUTLEDGE in association with GSE Research*, 23(3), 2017:23-53.

Pathak, Narendra Kumar. *Gender justice and law: a gender-specific study of landownership in uttarakhand*", Understanding Women's Land Rights: Gender Discrimination in Ownership, 13(2), 2017: 376.

Starr, Christian, Eileen, Lonz & Sandra Bern's Gender Schema Theory after 34 years: A review of its reach and impact. *A Journal of Educational Scientific Research*, 76(9), 2017: 566-578

Worsdale, Rewlon &Wright, John. *My objectivity is better than yours: contextualising debates about gender inequality*, Australia: Parkins Publishers, 2020, print.

Yunusa, Maxwell. Democratic Governance and Leadership in Nigeria: An Appraisal of the Challenges. *Lapai Luter National Journal of Management and Social Sciences*, 2 (1), 2019: 166-172.

Women and Change Expedition in Julie Okoh's *Edewede*
Eziwho Emenike AZUNWO

Abstract

Typically, perpetrated by stern patriarchal structure established since the times of old, the African society is jam-packed with oppressive and retrogressive customs and values that repress women. As a result, dramatists, especially, African women writers have embraced literary forms and subjects that highlight these issues and advocate for their elimination from society. Adopting Ideal Feminine as a theoretical framework, this paper interrogates Julie Okoh's *Edewede* with a view of revealing its impact in rousing her female characters from subjugation, ignorance and passivity, and to revolt against oppression through social protest. It is discovered that patriarchy is in many cases responsible for bringing about breaches in women's right and consequently propagating sexes imbalance. It is also discovered that education, consciousness-raising, sisterhood, female solidarity and resilience are powerful tools for women's empowerment in the play. It is therefore recommended that women should not be context bound in their choice and expression of feminist perspectives. The government both federal and traditional must look into traditions that are oppressive to the female folk. Society should be open to contemporary avenues and progressive choices that will pave the way for women social freedoms. A full-blown egalitarian human society is the ultimate dream.

Keywords: Drama, Feminism, Social Protest, Women's Right.

Introduction

Through the path of at least a century, the debate over the role, status, and position of women in the society of mankind has been willfully carried out in various ramifications across a density of areas. This debate is in fact full of depth, as it is complex, large and seemingly infinite. Typically characterized with grit, might and poise, these resounding qualities has for long given weight to this discourse so much so, the 19th century bore host to the spontaneous delivery of what could be characterized as a resilient movement; one popularly known today as, feminism.

Obviously idealistically, feminism is symptomatically built with the principal aim of ensuring social balance between the male and female sexes. Known to have begun in the USA, feminism soon spread like wild fire touching every corner of the earth. Such rare courage has not only caused a convolution of the feminist idea, but has in equal sense engendered various brands of feminism. Liberal feminism, African feminism, Marxist feminism, Radical feminism, Cultural feminism etc. are common brands of feminism. And although, each of the brand addresses feminism from a unique perspective, they all bear in them the feminist manifesto.

It is safe to say that feminism has pulled daring strings and consequently caused changes in a positive direction. Hence, today, in many societies that hitherto would not allow women work in public spaces, engage in politics or revolt against certain conditions that infringed on their rights and womanhood, women feel freer and happier to say the least. However, despite the effort of feminism plus other social, governmental and non-governmental institutions and agencies pressing hard to ensure that women are allowed to be completely expressive of their rights and privileges and to secure a society where there is comprehensive equality between sexes, women still appear to be second to men in almost all affairs, including social and domestic. As a result, the quest for women's right remains a stiff concern especially within the confines of gender discourses. However, noting that social protest is one superb method by which a group or sect can smear in seeking fairness in any socio-political space, this paper is therefore looking to appraise Julie Okoh's *Edewede* as a deserving commentary on the subject of women's right and gender imbalance. It is however hoped that in the context of this discourse, achieving an egalitarian society can be put on sight.

Précis of *Edewede*

Stanch to the abolishment of female circumcision, *Edewede* situates the activist, Edewede, and her immediate surrounding as an operative microcosm. Thus, being at the centre of attention, Edewede who had already suffered great pain following the loss of a couple of loved ones including her older sister and daughter, Ize, to the excesses of circumcision, is ready to sacrifice anything to prevent her daughter, Oseme, from participating in the initiation ceremony. However, Edewede's mother-in-law, Ebikere, is obdurately soaked in the traditions and customs of the land thus, expects Oseme to participate in the forthcoming initiation ceremony where she will be circumcised.

Unbending and particularly resolute as well in ensuring the opposite, Edewede prefers to go on loggerhead with Ebikere just to ensure that Oseme do not partake in the circumcision ritual. After the loss of Ize, Edewede learns from Eriala (Mama Nurse) the dangers of female circumcision. In fighting this cause, for support, Edewede involves her friend, Ebungbe, Eriala and consequently, the entire woman in the village excluding aged women who are predisposed to rather stay jammed with old traditions.

Eventually, after hosting a successful rally against female circumcision, the aged women and elders sanctioned a repudiation against Edewede for daring to desecrate an old served tradition. Ordia is thus forced to disconnect from his wife, Edewede, as she is banished from the village. In quick succession, the women in agreement left their homes not minding their husbands nor children and undertake a voluntary exile in a not too far land and remained in strike for seven long weeks.

The men and all that is left in the village feels deeply the women's absence. Consequently, following a democratic review of the matter by the elders and other men of the village, they conclude that their wives and mothers suspend the strike and return home. To the delight of everyone, the women are received back home in a grand style. Upon their arrival, the King publicly abolish female circumcision and even went further to sanction a death penalty to any defaulter. Specifically, Edewede return and her repudiation denounced makes Ordia a happy man and a proud husband.

Theoretical Framework

Bearing in mind the topic under scrutiny, the theory that serves as a model for which this work will be analyzed is the "ideal feminine". Basically, the basic precepts of this theory can be summarized in the works of Simone de Beauvoir and Betty Friedan. It however is important to note that the concept of femininity is pivotal to this discourse. Femininity can thus be viewed as the attributes, behaviours, interests, mannerisms, appearances, roles, and expectations that we have come to associate with being female during the socialization processes.

According to Yesiebo, "gender role socialization relies on modeling and reinforcement. Hence, girls and women learn and internalize socially expected and acceptable feminine traits and behaviours and are rewarded for gender-appropriate behavior" (Yesiebo 13). The ideal feminine has been discoursed for centuries. Citing Woolf, "women have served all these centuries as looking-glasses possessing the magic and delicious power of reflecting the figure of man at twice its natural size" (64).

Woolf's assertion in the fore clearly corroborates Simone de Beauvoir's point that women are the "other." To be specific, Beauvoir points out that:

> Man can think of himself without woman. She cannot think of herself without man. And she is simply what man decrees; thus called the sex", by which is meant that... she is sex – absolute sex, no less. She is defined and differentiated with

reference to man and not he with reference to her; she is the incidental, the inessential as opposed to the essential. He is the subject; he is the Absolute – she is the other (Beauvoir, 66).
Corroborating this thought, Betty Friedan, in her *The Feminine Mystique* also comments on the subject of the ideal feminine. Characteristically an idealistic essay, precisely, Friedan maintains that:

> The Feminine Mystique permits, even encourages, women to ignore the question of their identity. The mystique says they can answer the question Who am I? "by saying, Tom's wife... Mary's mother." – an American woman no longer has a private image to tell her who she is, or can be, or wants to be and that women are not considered female if they do not abide by these societal norms and mores. Friedan thinks that "the core of the problem for women today is not sexual but a problem of identity – a stunting or evasion of growth that is perpetuated by the feminine mystique (Friedan, 67).

Although, the idea of Friedan and the others referenced hitherto are closely expressive of the issues of gender role especially of relating to women's sexuality and womanhood, other related theories are concerned with the generality of sexes' imbalance.

Be that as it may, bearing in mind that the concept of feminist theory is relating to sex, gender, race, discrimination, equality, difference, and choice, Egbert and Sanders, expresses the view that there are systems and structures in place that work against individuals based on these qualities and against equality and equity.

Specifically, the latter notes that "research in critical paradigms requires the belief that, through the exploration of these existing conditions in the current social order, truths can be revealed. More important, however, this exploration can simultaneously build awareness of oppressive systems and create spaces for diverse voices to speak for themselves" (Egbert & Sanders, 12). Similarly, the idea here is to look at principal models that seeks to open grounds for balance amongst sexes in areas where lopsidedness is clearly evident.

Granted the foregoing, it becomes unequivocal to state that feminism is concerned with the constructs of intersectionality, dimensions of social life, social inequality, and social transformation. Therefore, in terms of theoretical application, it suffices to say that there are many potential ways to utilize this model in both theory and practice. It is fair to begin by analyzing what systems of power exist in a given society for instance. How do these systems work to create discrimination and exclusion? Becomes another indispensable step. Following a critical consideration of existing social structures, acknowledging barriers and issues inherit in the system becomes more or less an easy task. Consequently, it is on course to say that once these issues are acknowledged, they can be disrupted so that understanding and change can begin.

Women's Change Expedition in Julie Okoh's *Edewede*
Issues of women's right, gender imbalance and other related feministic issues has been a recurring decimally in both Western and Nigerian drama. In fact, from the classical dramas of Euripedes, Sophocles and Aristophanes, feminism has been a visible subject in

drama. The most prominent reflection of the feminist vision is that portrayed by Aristophanes in Lysistrata where the women of Athens and Sparta unite and embark on a sex strike in order to compel their husbands to end one nonsense Peloponnesian war. Interestingly, Aristophanes' play could have inspired a handful of plays with similar plot. One of such plays is J.P. Clark's *The Wives Revolt* and later, Barclays Ayakoroma's *Dance on His Grave*.

Drawing from the Aristophanes' model, these plays portray the agitation and struggle by the women for equal or fair treatment from their male counterparts who function as their husbands and fathers. In both plays i.e. *The Wives Revolt* and *Dance on His Grave*, the women drawn from various Niger Delta communities, resort to sex strike and decline from domestic chores as they embark on a self- imposed exile as a way of registering their protest over the denial of their self-worth by the men. Julie Okoh takes a similar cue from Aristophanes in the crafting of her masterpiece *Edewede* where the heroine of the play mobilizes the women in her community and embarks on exile as a way of protesting against female genital mutilation. In similar vein, like the victories recorded in Aristophanes' *Lysistrata*, Clark's *Wives Revolt* and Ayakoroma's *Dance on His Grave*, Okoh's women succeed in their protest as the King abolishes the practice of female circumcision in the community.

Raising the notion that the subject of human right is largely highlighted, Okoh in *Edewede* specifically questions the issue of the right of the girl child and abuse as portrayed through the means of a mandatory circumcision on Oseme, a teenager. It suffices to say that by virtue of being part of a human community, Oseme is imbued with some inalienable rights. Such rights include the right to be protected from harm or torture. Ironically, her rights are abused at the altar of primordial cultural values that sanction female circumcision as a law.

As a teenager who is capable of making her own choices, Oseme is opposed to the idea of female circumcision just like her mother, but rather than respect her views, her father, Ordia, boosted by her grand-mother, Ebikere, persuades her to present herself for circumcision without due consideration of the possible risks involved in it. Be that as it may, the significance of girl child rights in the play lies in the fact that, as a teenager, Oseme is expected to enjoy socio-cultural protection from her parents and other members of the community. In fact, one would expect that her family, which is her first constituency, should be responsible for the protection of her human rights. Ironically, her entire family except her mother, deny her such protection. It is actually her grand-mother, Ebikere, that instigates the entire process of trying to sanction her circumcision. Quite early in the play, Ebikere reminds her of the need for her to submit herself to be circumcised, thus:

> EBIKERE: Circumcision is part of our culture. My mother was circumcised. So also were her grand-mothers, great grand-mothers and great, great, great grand-mothers. It is a rite that every woman in this land goes through (Okoh, 2).

Ebikere's line of thought above clearly indicates that culture and tradition remain weapons deployed by men in most African societies to consistently cage and suppress women. Ebikere does not advance any reasonable logic or advantages of circumcision to drive her point but only begs the question that her ancestors did it and so it is justified.

However, even though Ebikere's insistence on circumcision can be understood against the background that she represents an age long tradition, Ordia's position appears quite absurd considering the fact that he has had a fair taste of modern life on account of education and exposure. Besides, as Oseme's father, he is naturally bound to protect his daughter from any form of harm be it cultural or religious. Ordinarily, Ordia is expected to be proactive in the protection of his only surviving daughter, Oseme, given the credit that he had lost his first daughter, Ize to health complications brought about after a circumcision exercise. Edewede recounts her horrible experience of circumcision:

> I was seized with fear, and my fear increased as I matured in age. Then came over turn to face the evil blade we all walked to the initiation camp but some never walked back from there. Akalo died to death; Denowe died few weeks later. As season rolled by, many more maidens passed away for the same cause, others remain destroyed for life" (Okoh, 18).

Ironically, Ordia prefers to sing the circumcision song along with his aged mother as he beckons on Oseme to surrender herself to be circumcised. Overwhelmed by the gory imageries she has experienced over circumcision, Edewede rises to the occasion and stops Oseme from being circumcised. However, characteristic of most African men, Ordia feels unrestraint to intimidate his wife by reminding her of the patriarchal cliché that he is her superior by virtue of being her husband. As Ordia puts it:

ORDIA: Wede! I am your husband. It is my duty to protect you too. So, listen to my advice. Do not allow that painful experience to becloud your reason. Give up this suicidal idea of yours (Okoh, 23).

Ordia's boast as the man of the house above smacks of infringements on the fundamental human rights of Edewede since he thinks that he is the only one capable of thinking and therefore must be listened to against all odds. The abuse of women's human rights in the play trickles down to the point where Edewede engages Ebikere, her mother-in-law in war of tongues. Amidst their heated verbal exchange, Ebikere reminds Edewede that her place in society is in the kitchen. "You don't even know that you are only a wife in this house. And as such, your place is in the kitchen" (Okoh, 7). Beyond the already said, there is more evidence to show that the structure of the African society is boldly built on patriarchal foundations. Drawing and playing the strereotypical card on women, relegating them to be background, as objects to be seen and not heard. With *Edewede*, Okoh however questions such reality with a decent appraisal of social protest.

In African societies, social protest has fondly been regarded as men's thing. Granted that men are mostly akin to engage in matters beyond the domestic parlance, the general perception is that politics and social protest are exclusively reserved for males alone. Well, truthfully, this has been the situation with Africans for a very long time, but whether this practice is correct or not is what millions of women across hundreds and thousands of traditional societies have hardly had the courage to question. In *Edewede*, Okoh did not only question that sort of chauvinistic routine, the latter equally found the grace to skillfully, intelligently and effectively debunk it.

Speaking in perspective, with the dimension of *Edewede's* plot and its final resolve, it becomes unequivocal to make the saying that as much as men have peculiar issues, so does women. And as men extemporaneously feel the itchiness to standup and challenge some of these issues, so does women too. Women have all the resources just like their male counterpart to fight any fight and make useful changes, however, their limitations surround fear, patriarchal forces and as well as the force of traditions. More so, at the very least, women lack the will-power and determination to stand sturdily for a course. However, with Edewede exercising great qualities, Okoh hopes to change the common narrative that women are weak, powerless and uninfluential. Speaking in context however, *Edewede* can thus be felt as a bright light uncovering those hidden qualities and capabilities women possesses. The need for women to effectively utilize their inborn qualities to speak up, fight and achieve great things is equally a significant lesson deducible from *Edewede*.

Way Forward

There are lots of issues affiliated with the girl child and women in Nigeria and they exist majorly through the lenses of ignorance and poverty, traditions and culture and patriarchy and gender stereotyping. However, while the rights of the girl child and women have been basically trampled upon through patriarchal traditions, female genital mutilation, child/early marriage, rape and sexual assault, domestic violence are some of the major issues resulting from sexes' imbalance. This situation is bad, touching and should be shunned. This paper therefore advocates for the freedom of the women folks even from the level of childhood. It suffices to say that before being a woman, every individual of the female gender is first and foremost a human being thus, as every man requires freedom of choice and of expression, every woman, beginning from their childhood deserves the same right. This paper therefore concludes on the note that the life of the girl child and of women in general is not limited by any means and as such, the society ought to lend them sufficient space to be fully expressive of themselves.

Works Cited
Beauvoir, Simone de. *The Second Sex*. Vintage Books. ISBN 978-0-09-959573-1. OCLC 1105756674. 2011

Egbert, J. & Sanden, S. *Foundations of Education Research: Understanding Theoretical Components*. Taylor & Francis. 2019.

Friedan, Betty. *The Feminine Mystique*. U. S. A: W.W.Noorton and Co. 1963.
John Ebimobowei Yeseibo. Female Self-Definition and Determination in Tsitsi Dangarembga's *She No Longer Weeps*. *Review of Arts and Humanities*, Vol. 7, No. 2, pp. 11-16. 2018. ISSN: 2334-2927 (Print), 2334-2935 (Online)

Okoh, Julie. *Edewede*. Totan Publishers. 2000. Print

Woolf, Virginia. *A Room of One's Own*. England: Hogart Press. 1929

Wollstonecraft, Mary. *A Vindication of the Rights of Women*. New York: Prometheus Books, 1989

Mmap Multi-disciplinary Series

If you have enjoyed *WRITING WOMAN ANTHOLOGY: Drama and Scholarly Essays*, consider these other fine books in the **Mmap Multi-disciplinary Series** from *Mwanaka Media and Publishing:*

Africanization and Americanization Anthology Volume 1, Searching for Interracial, Interstitial, Intersectional and Interstates Meeting Spaces, Africa Vs North America by Tendai R Mwanaka
A Conversation…, A Contact by Tendai Rinos Mwanaka
Africa, UK and Ireland: Writing Politics and Knowledge Production Vol 1 by Tendai R Mwanaka
Writing Language, Culture and Development, Africa Vs Asia Vol 1 by Tendai R Mwanaka, Wanjohi wa Makokha and Upal Deb
Zimbolicious: An Anthology of Zimbabwean Literature and Arts, Vol 3 by Tendai Mwanaka
Drawing Without Licence by Tendai R Mwanaka
Writing Grandmothers/ Escribiendo sobre nuestras raíces: Africa Vs Latin America Vol 2 by Tendai R Mwanaka and Felix Rodriguez
Tiny Human Protection Agency by Megan Landman
Ghetto Symphony by Mandla Mavolwane
A Portrait of Defiance by Tendai Rinos Mwanaka
Nationalism: (Mis)Understanding Donald Trump's Capitalism, Racism, Global Politics, International Trade and Media Wars, Africa Vs North America Vol 2 by Tendai R Mwanaka
Ouafa and Thawra: About a Lover From Tunisia by Arturo Desimone
Zimbolicious: An Anthology of Zimbabwean Literature and Arts, Vol 4 by Tendai Mwanaka and Jabulani Mzinyathi
Chitungwiza Mushamukuru Anthology by Tendai Rinos Mwanaka

The Day and the Dweller: A Study of the Emerald Tablets by Jonathan Thompson
Zimbolicious: An Anthology of Zimbabwean Literature and Arts, Vol 5 by Tendai Mwanaka
Robotics Anthology, Africa vs Asia Vol 2 by Tendai Rinos Mwanaka
Shaping Up by Tendai Rinos Mwanaka
Zimbolicious Anthology Vol 6: An Anthology of Zimbabwean Literature and Arts by Tendai Rinos Mwanaka and Chenjerai Mhondera
Registers of Loss: PhotoTalking to the Baobab Trees of Nyatate by Tendai Rinos Mwanaka
The Trick is to Keep Breathing: Covid 19 Stories From African and North American Writers, vol 3 by Tendai Rinos Mwanaka
Fixing Earth: An Anthology of Ireland, UK and Africa Writers, Vol 2 by Tendai Rinos Mwanaka
Zimbolicious: An Anthology of Zimbabwean Literature and Arts, Vol 7 Tendai Rinos Mwanaka and Tanaka Chidora

Upcoming
Writing Woman Anthology: Personal Essays and Short stories, An Anthology of African and Asian Writers, Vol 3 by Tendai Rinos Mwanaka, Abigail George, Sue Zhu and Mona Lisa Jena
WRITING WOMAN ANTHOLOGY: Poetry and Visual art, An Anthology of African and Asian Writers, Vol 3 by Tendai Rinos Mwanaka, Abigail George, Sue Zhu and Mona Lisa Jena

https://facebook.com/MwanakaMediaAndPublishing/

www.ingramcontent.com/pod-product-compliance
Lightning Source LLC
Chambersburg PA
CBHW051112230426
43667CB00014B/2549